Innovation Management

Innovation is the means by which organizations survive and thrive in uncertain and turbulent conditions. Innovation management has become a well-established field of research, teaching and practice, with a substantial literature. As a broad-based research field, contributions stem from an array of perspectives including science, economics, engineering and psychology. Innovation is crucial for economic and social progress, and it needs to be managed in order to be beneficial.

Innovation Management: A Research Overview provides a concise introduction to the best research on innovation management. It covers four main themes: foundational studies, concepts and frameworks, important empirical studies, and current and emerging themes. The research discussed includes classic studies, with core insights in the field, key thinking on strategies and processes for innovation, well-established and novel research methods, and issues of greatest contemporary importance.

This shortform book provides direction through the maze of research on the nature, processes and outcomes of innovation management, and provides an invaluable introduction to the literature on innovation management for students and professionals.

Mark Dodgson is Professor of Innovation Studies at the University of Queensland Business School, and Visiting Professor at Imperial College London. He has written or edited 16 books and over 100 academic articles on innovation, and has researched and taught innovation in over 60 countries.

State of the Art in Business Research
Edited by Professor Geoffrey Wood

Recent advances in theory, methods and applied knowledge (alongside structural changes in the global economic ecosystem) have presented researchers with challenges in seeking to stay abreast of their fields and navigate new scholarly terrains.

State of the Art in Business Research presents shortform books which provide an expert map to guide readers through new and rapidly evolving areas of research. Each title will provide an overview of the area, a guide to the key literature and theories and time-saving summaries of how theory interacts with practice.

As a collection, these books provide a library of theoretical and conceptual insights, and exposure to novel research tools and applied knowledge, that aid and facilitate in defining the state of the art, as a foundation stone for a new generation of research.

Innovation Management
A Research Overview
Mark Dodgson

Innovation Management
A Research Overview

Mark Dodgson

Routledge
Taylor & Francis Group

LONDON AND NEW YORK

First published 2018
by Routledge
2 Park Square, Milton Park, Abingdon, Oxon OX14 4RN

and by Routledge
711 Third Avenue, New York, NY 10017

Routledge is an imprint of the Taylor & Francis Group, an informa business

British Library Cataloguing-in-Publication Data
A catalogue record for this book is available from the British Library

Library of Congress Cataloging-in-Publication Data
A catalog record for this book has been requested

ISBN: 978-0-8153-7529-6 (hbk)
ISBN: 978-1-351-24018-5 (ebk)

Typeset in Times New Roman
by Apex CoVantage, LLC

Contents

1 Introduction

It is very common nowadays to hear the word 'innovation' in the speeches of business leaders and politicians. The innovation strategies of firms and innovation policies of governments aim to improve corporate and national capacities to be innovative, thereby to achieve desired aims such as enhanced competitiveness, productivity, growth and profitability. It is therefore recognized as an important concern, but what is meant by innovation, and importantly how can it be managed to assure the outcomes sought? Innovation is a term used very broadly, and is commonly misused. On the one hand, it refers to revolutionary changes, such as the internet, and on the other, small incremental changes, such as the latest version of an app. It is confused and conflated with issues such as invention and creativity that are important contributors to innovation, but missing an essential definitional element: innovation is the successful *application* of new ideas. Because many attempts to innovate fail, innovation is also something that often requires some form of intervention in its encouragement and formulation, and the way it is managed is critical to its success. There is a huge variety of approaches and tools for its management, and there are many issues surrounding their appropriateness. So innovation and its management are matters that are hugely important, but are also contentious and problematic and therefore require deep analysis and understanding. This book offers an overview of the core academic literature on innovation and its management, highlighting the implications this literature has for the practice of innovation.

The book will draw on the author's lengthy experience of researching and teaching innovation, and his experience of advising companies and governments on its encouragement and application. This interest in the subject goes back to his undergraduate degree, studying Society and Technology in 1974, and his PhD on innovation in small firms completed in 1984.

As well as writing numbers of books and articles on the subject, he has edited substantial volumes which have collected, in his opinion, the best broad-ranging thinking on innovation. These go back to *The Handbook of Industrial Innovation*, Mark Dodgson and Roy Rothwell (eds.), Cheltenham, Edward Elgar, 1994. More recently he co-edited *The Oxford Handbook of Innovation Management*, Mark Dodgson, David Gann and Nelson Phillips, Oxford, Oxford University Press, 2014, and the four-volume collection upon which this book mainly draws: Mark Dodgson, *Innovation Management: Critical Perspectives on Business and Management* (ed.), Volume 1, *Foundations*; Volume 2, *Concepts and Frameworks*; Volume 3, *Important Empirical Studies*; Volume 4, *Current and Emerging Themes*, London, Routledge, 2016. Although there were many important historical contributions to the field, over the past 40 years in particular there has been a massive increase in interest in innovation management. Imperfect though it might be, it is illustrative that a simple Google search of the term innovation management produces over 20 million results. It is the intention of this book to select within this universe of interest, and identify and explain the contributions that the author believes provide the most valuable insights into the issue of innovation and its management.

The study of innovation management is an applied field, driven by its practice. Diverse theories can, however, help explain various aspects of innovation management as a social and economic process. Psychology researchers can explain the motivations of innovative individuals, sociologists explain the power relationships between and within groups and organizations that affect innovation as a social endeavour, and political scientists enlighten the influences institutions can exert. Organization theorists explain how new fields of knowledge and effort are formed and institutionalized, and how practices are negotiated and become embedded. Without underestimating the contributions of these approaches, this book's focus is on the organization and on theories within economics and strategic management, with a common concern to explain how value from innovation is created, captured and deployed.

What is innovation, and why is its management important?

Innovation is the means by which organizations survive and thrive in uncertain and turbulent conditions. Technological change, globalization and changing patterns of consumption are compounding the complex and rapidly changing circumstances in which organizations operate. Innovation reflects the ability of organizations to understand, respond to and lead the changes needed to endure and succeed in such environments. Innovation contributes centrally to economic performance, corporate competitiveness, environmental sustainability, levels and nature of employment, and in the final analysis, overall quality of life. There are widespread social and economic benefits from innovation, but the organizational returns from it are skewed towards those better at managing its risks and complexities.

The challenges of innovation management are summarized by Dodgson, Gann and Phillips (2014: 3):

> The risks, costs, and timescales of innovation often conflict with the financial objectives, operational routines, and managerial incentives found in most organizations. The best returns to innovation may be accrued not by the innovator, but by those that emulate and copy. Innovation disrupts markets, technologies, and workplaces. It requires levels of collaboration across professional and organizational boundaries, and tolerance of failure, that organizations find difficult to coordinate and sanction. In many instances it involves efforts to manage activities and events that are beyond the control of even their most influential contributors.

At the same time, and despite these difficulties, they argue innovation can be the most stimulating and rewarding of all organizational activities.

Innovation does not happen automatically. The positive consequences of innovation result from its successful management, which can also mitigate some of its negative results. The positive consequences can include growth, competitiveness and productivity. Innovative organizations have energy and drive and can be fun and stimulating places to work in. The negative consequences can include loss of existing jobs, environmental damage and the debilitating effect of continual change and workplace insecurity.

Innovation is a very imprecise word. It is an *outcome* (a new service or way of organizing, for example) and a *process* (the way resources and capabilities are combined over time to produce innovative outcomes). Innovation can be radical, transformative and disruptive to existing ways of doing things, or it can be small, incremental steps in improving what is already being done: just doing things a little bit better. These wide-ranging differences have great significance for defining the scope of innovation management. In this book, the focus is on innovations that are substantially novel, and involve change and risk, as these are the most challenging and arguably the most consequential for organizations and management. The book considers innovations in products, services and processes, in ways of organizing and getting to the market, and in business models: the ways organizations construct the means to deliver value. Although the focus is mainly on the organization, consideration is given to the broader context in which they operate, such as nations, industries, sectors and technologies. Most of the research addressed here explores technological innovation, and while this is important in and of itself, it also holds lessons for other forms of innovation in the way it reveals some of the challenges and solutions of, for example, strategy formulation and implementation, organizational learning, and overcoming institutional rigidities and introspection.

Innovation management has become a well-established field of research, teaching and practice, with a substantial literature. Like innovation itself, innovation management is broad-based in the issues it addresses, ranging from its connection with science, on the one hand, to understanding of customers and markets on the other. It is concerned with research and development (R&D) and new product and service development, and the supportive organizational forms and practices, and strategies, which create, capture and deliver value from innovation. It is studied by, among others, economists, management and business academics, engineers, geographers, psychologists, organization theorists, intellectual property lawyers and those who increasingly identify as working in the field of innovation studies.

Innovation has become a central interest for firms and organizations, with regular reference to their development of innovation strategies and processes. There are innovation directors and managers, innovation committees and boards, innovation budgets and prizes. Yet there is considerable variation in what these various initiatives constitute and their quality. Similarly, there has been a significant increase in the number of consultants proffering advice on innovation, with markedly different levels of competence. Within academia, innovation has become a core interest, especially in the business and management fields, yet questions arise about the depth of expertise possessed by some of those purporting to research and teach in the area. This all points to the need to recognize and appreciate the foundations and core aspects of the field, an endeavour to which this book aims to contribute.

The book covers well-established 'classic' articles, and some newer research judged to be helpful and influential. Innovation management, like much management research, is prone to trends and over-excitement about the 'next big thing'. The focus here is on robust, insightful research; it assumes that there is much to be learned from the past, and the best contemporary thinking about innovation is cognizant of and builds upon accumulated knowledge. The book aims to provide direction through the maze of research on the nature, processes and outcomes of innovation management, and will be an invaluable source for those studying and researching the subject.

Chapter 2 addresses prominent foundational articles in the area, upon which the field has built. Many have a historical basis. There is considerable value in scholars reflecting on the lessons from history, and considering the present and future challenges of innovation management in the light of those lessons. Many are written by economists, and while they are very critical of the ability of conventional neo-classical economics to explain innovation, the insights these economists provide are very revealing of the macro forces that influence the formation and direction of innovation. This chapter considers the dynamics of innovation, the forces behind it and their outcomes, and the different types of innovation. The difficulties of innovation will be considered: how the diffusion of new ideas can be slow, how the best technology does not always win, how organizations often resist it, and at a more macro level, how politics and culture can constrain it. It analyzes the importance of collaboration and social networks for innovation, and the strategic and managerial challenges of innovation and how they have been confronted.

Chapter 3 introduces some of the major analytical tools in the field. There is no theory of innovation management, but there are some useful frameworks and concepts. These range from the somewhat abstract and aggregate (i.e. discontinuities and disruption) to generic analytical tools (i.e. absorptive capacity, dynamic capabilities, complementary assets, appropriability, core capabilities and core rigidities) to specific means for managing innovation (i.e. lead users, brokerage, stage gate systems, teams and platforms). The chapter will also include concepts that help us better understand the nature of innovation, such as architectural innovation and markets for technology, and the features of innovations that further their diffusion and imitation, including organizational learning. It also includes reference to the new tool of social network analysis.

Chapter 4 includes a selection of the most important empirical studies, both quantitative and qualitative (case studies). The research methods used range from econometric analysis of large databases to rich explanations of the contributions of individuals. Contributions reflect on the shortcomings of their various data sources, and there remain some profound difficulties in empirical studies of innovation management. Some of the earliest empirical studies revealed sectoral differences in the challenges of innovation, and these remain crucially important determinants of innovation management practice. Research shows the important contributions of science and marketing, of entrepreneurship and building on existing institutions. It reveals the importance of organizational culture and leadership, different organizational forms, and measuring the returns to innovation. This chapter also addresses the innovation management issues associated with intellectual property, technical standards, and mergers and acquisitions.

Chapter 5 addresses the most current topical issues in innovation management and its future challenges. It considers 'open', 'business model' and 'inclusive' innovation, and the question of 'design-led' innovation. Innovation is considered in service sectors, social innovation and large complex projects, and in its relationship with corporate and environmental sustainability. The way that technology is affecting the ways innovation is managed is addressed, as are the different patterns of innovation management we are seeing in new important players in Asia, Latin America and elsewhere. An enduring lesson of innovation management is that it is a global activity and its good practice can be found all around the world.

In a final reflection in this introduction, it is possible to speculate upon the influence that the study of innovation has had more broadly on the study of business and management. Certainly the subject has attracted interest from a wide range of management academics, from among others strategy, organizational behaviour, international business, marketing, finance and accounting, and information systems. It is presumptuous to claim that innovation management has changed these areas of study, but it is perhaps justifiable to suggest that there are certain elements of its study which may be interesting for other areas to reflect upon and consider their comparative performance (if only to confirm their superiority). The first is that innovation management is deeply engrained in practice, and although there are some fundamentals which haven't changed over time, the practice of innovation changes rapidly. Understanding and theorizing in the field therefore requires deep engagement with current structures and processes. Second, and relatedly, innovation is fundamentally complex and uncertain, and hence there is a need to account for emergence, disruption, evolution and non-scalability.

When management studies address phenomena that are unpredictable and unstable, there are perhaps lessons from those that study innovation, for whom these conditions are normal. Third, the field emphasizes the centrality of collaboration between and within organizations. As this often involves combinations of different capabilities and perspectives (i.e. scientific/technological, operational and marketing), it necessitates an interdisciplinary approach. Explanations from within particular disciplinary boundaries are likely to be limiting. Fourth, innovation management is shaped by the interaction between levels of analysis, and recognition that what occurs within the organization is deeply affected by its external environment (and occasionally vice versa). This not only includes issues such as forces of competition, industry dynamics, geography, and policy settings, but also changing patterns of consumption and broader social attitudes. Innovation management requires rich, diverse and evolving interpretation, with the lesson for any study of management that is restricted, narrow and static that it has yet to catch up with contemporary realities.

2 Foundational studies

This chapter is concerned with some of the foundational thinking about the nature of innovation and some core ideas about its management. As an economic phenomenon, innovation is different. Brian Arthur (1990), in his article "Positive feedbacks in the economy", makes the profoundly important point that in contrast to the conventional view in economics about diminishing returns to investment (plant and equipment wear out, competitive advantages diminish over time), in areas of high technology and innovation there are *positive feedbacks* and *increasing returns*. That is, investment in knowledge and innovation increases opportunities for further knowledge and innovation. The more a product or technology is used, the more it improves and more attractive it becomes. Furthermore, the paths of progress are nonlinear and can be locked in by random events, making things highly dynamic and unpredictable. Just because a product is the best technically does not mean it will succeed in the market: there are just too many intervening variables. Arthur equates the traditional view of economics being akin to Newtonian physics, predictable and linear, and contrasts it with modern physics or evolutionary theory, where paths of development are complex, uncertain and subject to randomness. Fundamental to understanding innovation management is appreciation of the complexity and uncertainty that surrounds it.

The implications of positive feedbacks for innovation management are that investments in innovation, unlike investing in a factory or information technology (IT) infrastructure that dates and deteriorates, are capable of growing their contributions over time. However, those contributions are subject to many uncertainties, requiring astute management of innovation.

From a macro perspective, innovation can be seen to follow distinctive paths or patterns. James Utterback's (1994) work on "The dynamics of innovation in industry" is a revealing examination of technical advance using the case of the *waves of progress* from the development of manual typewriters to electric typewriters to word processors to personal computers. He reveals a number of characteristics of each transition. Each new capability drew on old capabilities, combining existing components. This reflects the classic view of the economist Joseph Schumpeter (1934) that innovation consists of *new combinations*. Utterback describes how each transition is accompanied by a *shifting ecology* of firms, with swarms of new entrants, few of which survive, and which results in new leaders in the industry. He also points out that the technology brought into the innovation may come from another industry or sector, which adds to the disruption experienced by incumbents.

One of the major contributions of Utterback's work is the concept of the *dominant design*. At the early stages of an innovation's development there can be numerous competing designs and configurations that over time crystallize into one dominant version. The IBM personal computer, for example, became the classic model of how that product was configured. Utterback also points to the profound social consequences of innovation, showing how changes in the technology of putting print on paper provided massive new job opportunities for women, moving them from the farm into offices that were previously solely occupied by men. Joseph Schumpeter (1942) characterized innovation as *creative destruction*, and it is always to be remembered that the creativity of innovation, with new products, firms, industries and jobs, is mirrored by the destruction of those they replace, with profound consequences for those affected.

Utterback briefly tells the story of the development of the QWERTY keyboard, and this is further developed in work by Paul David (1985) in his article "Clio and the economics of QWERTY". In David's study he poses the question why QWERTY continues to be the dominant keyboard layout, when another configuration, the Dvorak layout, is proven to be faster and more efficient. One of the answers lies in the way the keyboard is part of a larger production system ranging from the manufacture of typewriters and personal computers to the training programmes used to give people the skills to use them. This combination of numerous elements – technical relatedness, economies of scale, and patterns of learning and habituation – locks in early configurations, making them irreversible without substantial costs. Thus, the first 'dominant design' to emerge may not intrinsically be the best, and may have been influenced by chance events, but it creates a *path dependent trajectory* that constrains the direction of the technology's development.

The issue of path dependency is featured in "Technological paradigms and technological trajectories" by Giovanni Dosi (1982), one of the most highly cited papers in economics. Drawing on the concept of *technological trajectories* of Richard Nelson and Sidney Winter (1982) and the understanding of *paradigms* of Thomas Kuhn (1962), Dosi argues how patterns of innovation follow cumulative paths in which experiments and learning generate bounded knowledge which is technology and firm specific and creates different rates of technological progress. The considerable impact of this paper is discussed in Von Tunzelmann, Malerba, Nightingale and Metcalfe (2008), and its consequences for the management of innovation include focusing attention on organization and capabilities in the firm, and the ways that investments in research are by themselves insufficient causes of innovation.

These works are illustrative of some of the foundations of the study of innovation and its management. One of the foundational figures in the field, and for many the father of contemporary studies of innovation, Christopher Freeman (1994), produced an extended critique on "The economics of technical change". It provides a comprehensive and critical study of the state of knowledge about the economics of technical change and a wide-ranging review of the fundamental understanding of innovation. Freeman's first observation is how economists generally deal badly with innovation. Traditional economic theories, models and measurements cannot capture the *uncertainty, complexity and evolutionary nature of innovation*. Schumpeter is preeminent among economists who do include innovation centrally in their work, and he began his analysis by emphasizing the central role of the entrepreneur (Schumpeter, 1934). Freeman shows how Schumpeter's views changed over time as he came to recognize the contributions made by large organizations with formal research and development (R&D) departments. Crucially, Schumpeter extolled the virtues of studying companies to understand how innovation actually occurs in practice, and in amending theories and models of innovation to reflect changing realities.

Freeman reviews the arguments over whether innovation results from the *technology push* of new technological developments or the *demand pull* of changing requirements of customers and markets, and shows how these alternatives are reconciled in *interactive models*. He examines the importance of external sources of technology: users, suppliers and networks of one kind or another, and the internal organizational advantages of linking R&D and production. Key to understanding patterns of innovation is appreciation of *industrial and sectoral differences*, for example in their connections with basic research and the extent to which they rely on incremental or radical innovations. Freeman analyzes the importance of institutions supporting innovation and the configuration of different national systems of innovation. One of his great strengths as an economist is his appreciation of managerial, organizational and behavioural factors influencing innovation, and he emphasizes the importance of continuous *interactive learning*.

It is important to understand sectoral differences and their influence on innovation management. Much research in the area in the 1980s, for example, focused particularly on the automotive industry, and there continues to be special interest in 'high-tech' sectors such as advanced engineering, information and communication technologies (ICT) and biotechnology. This has been balanced to some extent by the study of more traditional, but not necessarily less innovative, sectors such as construction. There still remains a comparative paucity of good studies of innovation management in service sectors, such as banking and insurance. Malerba and Adams (2014) discuss the important influence of sectoral differences on innovation management. Sectoral systems of innovation in ICT, for example, are in many ways unlike those in textiles. Using examples of pharmaceuticals, machine tools and services, Malerba and Adams provide a framework that links knowledge and sources of innovation with the actors and institutions involved to explain the dynamics of innovative activity within and across sectoral boundaries. This framework is a valuable addition to the innovation manager's toolbox in helping analyze the context in which their organizations innovate.

The widely diverse, emergent and complex nature of innovation has prevented the development of comprehensive theories that explain its nature. There are, however, useful models and insights that have great explanatory value. One such contribution is William Abernathy and James Utterback's (1975) "A dynamic model of process and product innovation". This model, which is empirically tested, explains the pattern of innovation within a firm according to the stage of development of its production process and its chosen basis of competition. The model suggests that *product* and *process* innovations evolve over time in a consistent and identifiable pattern. The authors do recognize, however, that progress can be intermittent, and it can pause and even reverse. They tie this evolutionary model to the strategy the firm pursues in response to its environment and whether it is focused on maximizing performance or sales or minimizing costs. The managerial implications of this model include understanding the kinds of innovation to be supported appropriate to the stage of development of the firm and its strategic objectives.

Keith Pavitt's (1991) paper on "Key characteristics of the large innovating firm" captures many of the insights from his extensive research into innovation and its management. He argues that large firms are important contributors to innovation, display considerable resilience and are characterized by specific, differentiated and cumulative technological development. Pavitt argues that firms' search for technology is constrained by what they have done in the past. That is, technical change is largely a cumulative process specific to individual firms. He argues the importance of organizing and orchestrating competences across functional, disciplinary and divisional boundaries, which involves continuous learning in various forms and a broad strategic approach to innovation. The paper includes reference what has become known as the Pavitt Typology of regular patterns differentiating between *specialized supplier, scale intensive, information intensive* and *science-based* sectors. These sectors have different sources and trajectories of technology, posing different strategic management of innovation and technology problems.

David Teece's (1986) "Profiting from technological innovation: Implications for integration, collaboration, licensing and public policy" is a true classic. His intention is to answer the question of why it so often happens that it is not the innovator that profits from their innovation, but competitors and imitators. Key to answering this question is access to *complementary assets.* These include marketing, competitive manufacturing and after sales support. He distinguishes between generic, specialized and cospecialized assets with different levels of dependence for the innovation. Other elements of Teece's approach include dominant designs and *appropriability regimes,* or the extent to which returns from innovations can be appropriated by patents or copyright or not, and whether the regimes are 'tight' or 'weak'. Among the implications of Teece's approach is explaining the conditions on when to contract externally and when to integrate in-house. Firms operating with weak appropriability and high dependence on complementary assets that they do not own, or have privileged access to, are unlikely to profit from innovation. Returns from investing in R&D are likely to be greater among firms with the assets in place that give them distinctive advantages in the commercialization of their innovations.

Wesley Cohen and Daniel Levinthal (1994) introduce the concept of *absorptive capacity* in their paper "Fortune favors the prepared firm". They argue that the ability of a firm to recognize the value of new external information, and then assimilate and apply it, is crucial for its ability to innovate. This absorptive capacity largely results from the firm's level of prior related knowledge, and lack of previous investments may foreclose opportunities for developing technical capability. Learning and problem-solving skills tend to more effective when they are related to what is already known, which accentuates the path dependency of innovation. Cohen and Levinthal contend that individuals absorb external knowledge and, with effective communications, organizations can absorb more than the totality of the individuals in them.

A key insight from Cohen and Levinthal is that firms invest in R&D not only to generate new knowledge, but also to increase their capacity to absorb knowledge. R&D generates innovation and facilitates learning. This helps explain why firms invest in basic research, despite that research spilling out into the public domain. Their analysis suggests that because ease of learning is dependent on earlier experience in related areas, the diffusion and adoption of innovations depends on their propinquity to what is known. It also argues that cooperative ventures in novel rather than established areas require greater investments in absorptive capacities.

Roy Rothwell's (1994) "Towards the fifth-generation innovation process" analyzes generational changes that have occurred in the *processes* firms use to innovate. Rothwell's great contribution lay in his foresight about the way innovation was changing as a result of greater systemic integration and networking within and between firms and the application of new digital tools that lead to the 'electronification of innovation'. Rothwell's five generations include *technology push, market pull, 'coupling', integrated*, and *systems integrated and networking*. In the first two, the focus of the firm is to lead with technology or market insight. The coupling process is concerned with the communications in the firm that allow the meshing of technological and market opportunities. The integrated process has a more external orientation, to do with collaboration with customers and suppliers, but also draws on the experience of successful Japanese firms at the time, known for their highly integrated internal organization. It is the fifth-generation process where Rothwell's foresight comes to the fore, especially with his analysis of the digital connections possible between design and manufacture (this issue is discussed further in Chapter 5).

Deeply immersed in the practical realities of innovative firms, Rothwell writes about the trade-offs between speed and cost, and identifies 24 factors that underlie successful innovation. Although this approach has been criticized for assuming that each stage was 'better', Rothwell was careful to note that each generation of innovation process could occur concurrently. Rather than taking a generational approach, the different *models* of innovation Rothwell described underlie the non-temporal analysis of Dodgson, Gann and Phillips (2014), who add a sixth model – future ready – which includes consideration of environmental sustainability, a trend identified by Rothwell.

Research in innovation management has tended to focus much more on the creation of innovations rather than their subsequent *diffusion*. The most notable exception is Everett Rogers's (1995) magisterial book *The Diffusion of Innovations*. Among the many insights this work provides, Rogers argues that diffusion results from subjective evaluations of an innovation, derived from individuals' personal experiences and perceptions and conveyed by interpersonal networks. He describes five different attributes of innovation affecting their diffusion: *relative advantage, compatibility, complexity, trialability* and *observability*. Relative advantage – whether an innovation is better than what exists – includes issues of cost and profitability on the one hand, and status and prestige on the other. They include whether there are incentives (such as financial inducements) or mandates for adoption (such as environmental regulations). Compatibility is the degree to which an innovation complies with existing values, past experiences and future needs. Complexity refers to the degree to which an innovation is perceived to be difficult to understand and use. Trialability is the extent to which an innovation can be experimented with on a limited basis to dispel uncertainty. Observability is the extent to which the results of an innovation are visible to others. In addition to these five attributes, Rogers suggests other factors that affect diffusion include the type of innovation decision (whether it is made by an individual or an organization); the nature of the communication channels informing diffusion through the decision-making process; the nature of the social system, such as its norms; and the efforts of change agents promoting the innovation.

Of all the author's favourite studies of innovation, Elting Morison's (1988, original 1966) "Gunfire at sea" is a standout. It is a case study of diffusion, but it looks much more closely at the factors that limit diffusion and the organizational and personal factors that make it so hard for organizations to introduce novelty. The innovation – rapid and more accurate gunfire in the nineteenth century US and British navies – met all of Roger's criteria. It clearly had superior results, used existing technology and platforms, wasn't especially complex, and could be trialled and was observable. Yet the innovation was very slow to diffuse. Morison points to a number of reasons. It was introduced into an organization – the US Navy – that was very successful in winning all its wars, and saw no need to change. The idea for the innovation came from a junior ranked officer in a highly hierarchical organization and furthermore was sourced from a remote location far from where decisions were made. It is revealing that the innovation really only gained momentum when supported by US President Theodore Roosevelt, an experienced ex-soldier who had run the Navy Department, knowledgeable of military bureaucracy and fully aware of the advantages of accurately shooting at the enemy before they shoot at you. This case study endures because it continues to resonate powerfully today: organizations develop resolute inertias that limit innovation, and radical change inevitably involves the endorsement and support of senior leaders.

For many of the most profound and enduring insights into the whole discipline of management, one turns to Peter Drucker, and this also applies to his views on innovation. In "The discipline of innovation", Drucker (1985) writes that innovation is more about knowing than doing and involves the combination of hard work and inspiration. He describes seven areas of opportunity that managers should assess to guide innovation: unexpected occurrences, incongruities, process needs, industry and market changes, demographic changes, changes in perception and new knowledge. Some of these lie within the firm and some outside. For Drucker, purposeful, systematic innovation begins with analysis of these sources of new opportunity. He argues there is talent, ingenuity and knowledge behind innovation, but there is also hard, focused work. He also observes that if an innovation does not aim for leadership from the start, it is unlikely to be innovative enough.

Many of the deepest insights into innovation management have a long history, and this is seen in the work by Tom Burns and G. M. Stalker (1961) on "Mechanistic and organic systems of management". Based on research undertaken in the 1950s, their book *The Management of Innovation* asks some profound questions about the organization of work and its leadership, and raises continuingly important questions of how personal and institutional ambitions are reconciled within organizations. It is the distinction between *mechanistic* and *organic* systems for which Burns and Stalker are best remembered, with each appropriate to different rates of technical and commercial change experienced by the organization. Mechanistic management systems are appropriate to stable conditions, characterized, for example, by hierarchical structures of control, authority and communication, and precise definitions of roles and responsibilities. Organic forms are appropriate to changing conditions, where new and unforeseen problems arise that cannot be dealt with by hierarchy and strictly defined functions. They are characterized, for example, by the adjustment and continual redefinition of tasks and a network structure of control, authority and communication. Burns and Stalker discuss the difficulties and opportunities each system has for managers and workers. They make the important point that these two systems are not dichotomous, they are polarities, and organizations can vacillate between the two and indeed operate with both (a point rediscovered latterly in discussion of 'ambidextrous organizations', although they did not initiate the term; see, for example, Tushman and O'Reilly, 1996). The chapter concludes with the enduring insight that "The beginning of administrative wisdom is the awareness that there is no one optimum type of management system".

The view about the complexity and contingency of management decisions about innovation is echoed in Keith Pavitt's (1990) article on "What we know about the strategic management of technology". Pavitt's work was always strongly empirically based, commonly derived from the patent analysis conducted by his long-term collaborator, Pari Patel, and it allowed him to question a number of core assumptions in the strategic management literature. For example, Pavitt shows the normal strategic choices presumed to be made between breadth versus depth of technology investments, products versus processes, and leader versus follower strategies are strongly dependent on the firm's size and core business. He argues that 'history matters' and firms develop specific competences over time, and that their capacity to learn is crucially important in order to deal with the uncertainties that confront them. Pavitt also argues the importance of the *implementation* of technology strategy. While acknowledging the uncertainties of the planning processes behind innovation investments, and the deeply political nature of many decisions, Pavitt contend that the successful management of technology depends upon the capacity to orchestrate and integrate functional and specialist groups for the implementation of innovation, continuous questioning of existing strategies and structures, and a willingness to take a long-term view over technology accumulation.

Some of the focusing and integrative features of Pavitt's analysis remain when moving from the idea of technology strategy to the broader concept of innovation strategy. Innovation strategies involve decisions about how innovation supports overall organizational objectives and what innovations to pursue. They encourage high levels of internal and external organizational integration in support of overall corporate objectives, rather than individual projects, and this may involve investments in coordinating technological infrastructure and platforms. The ability to formulate and implement innovation strategy and encourage highly coordinated internal and external organizational support for innovation is a key management capability.

Andrew van de Ven (1986) offers a conceptual framework in his article on "Central problems in the management of innovation". His framework builds on four factors – new ideas, people, transactions and institutional context – and how their interrelations lead to *four basic problems* confronting general managers. The first is the human problem of managing attention when innovation is non-routine and complex. The second is the process problem of managing new ideas into good currency, which is getting them implemented and adopted. The third is the structural problem of integrating parts of the firm into a coherent whole. The fourth is the strategic management problem of institutional leadership. Van de Ven offers some speculations from the literature on how these problems can be addressed, and emphasizes factors such as experimentation and learning, organizational and functional integration, and leadership institutionalized in a culture and in organizational practices that accept uncertainty and complexity.

Innovation management researchers continually refer to the importance of the external context in which firms operate. One crucial component of that external context is the national system of innovation. In his paper "The 'national system of innovation' in historical perspective", Christopher Freeman (1995), one of the originators of the study of national systems of innovation, places them in historical context. He shows that historically there have been major differences between countries in the ways they have organized and sustained the development, introduction, improvement and diffusion of new products and processes within their national economies. Freeman's historical analysis goes back to the Industrial Revolution in Britain, and he charts the policies pursued by Germany and then the United States to learn and catch up with Britain's leadership. He latterly charts the strength of the Japanese system and contrasts the success of many East Asian countries compared to those in Latin America. The emphasis lies in *national* characteristics, as despite globalization and the growth of multinational companies, nations matter greatly, for example in the way they organize and fund their R&D, and on the *systemic* nature of the connections between the institutions supporting innovation. The work by Freeman and others on national innovation systems spawned a massive research interest among policy makers internationally and in organizations such as the Organisation for Economic Co-operation and Development (OECD).

Freeman discusses the shortcomings of Soviet Russia's national innovation system, and the differences between *socialist* and market *capitalist* approaches to innovation are brilliantly revealed in Bruce Kogut and Udo Zander's (2000) study of the Zeiss company: "Did socialism fail to innovate? A natural experiment of the two Zeiss companies". A company with a long history of technological excellence, Zeiss was split after World War Two, with one part in the Federal Republic of Germany (the capitalist West Germany) and the other in the German Democratic Republic (the socialist East Germany) and were subsequently reunified following the collapse of the Soviet bloc. This separation of some 40 years allowed Kogut and Zander to undertake a rare social science natural experiment, exploring by using patent analysis and interviews how the Zeiss company innovated under different political systems. They show that the Zeiss company in East Germany had considerable technical and managerial capabilities, but were hampered by a system of central planning that dissipated innovative resources in accordance with planned targets. The company was directed to produce for a wide range of customers, preventing the development of strategic focus. The central plan refused to permit experimentation in any sector of the economy for fear of failure, and this limited Zeiss's access to external innovations. Zeiss in East Germany also lacked close connections with advanced consumers and suppliers in many areas. Zeiss in East Germany did not lack internal incentives or abilities to innovate, but these were confined by a broader planned system incapable of providing the stimuli to innovate found in its counterpart company in West Germany.

The question of incentives is part of the answer to the great historical mystery of why China's global technological leadership dissipated after the fourteenth century. Joel Mokyr (1990) presents various answers to this question in his chapter "China and Europe" from his book *The Lever of Riches*. Mokyr lists the extraordinary range of technologies in which China was at the forefront until 1400: in agriculture; the production of iron and textiles; water power, and maritime technology. He then canvasses the range of suggestions about why this progress and leadership suddenly stopped. They range from the Confucian elevation of public administration and scholarship over trade to nutritional deficiencies in the population. Some argue the strong cultural and social affinity for harmony in China limited the opportunities for disruptive innovation, while others point to China's peculiar lack of progress in some branches of mathematics. Mokyr himself argues that a major difference between the technological stagnation in China and growth in post-Renaissance Europe was that in Europe, the power of any social group to sabotage an innovation deemed detrimental to its interests was far smaller. Smaller, fragmented nations with greater social diversity encouraged competition. Private interests in Europe had incentives to invest. In China, by contrast, there was high dependence on the state, and the elites running the government had little incentive to invest in technology and innovation. One of the foundational precepts of innovation is that diversity and competition are crucial ingredients for its stimulation.

In a final reflection on these contributions, it is worth considering whether they are foundational because of the quality of their research and exposition, or simply because they were published first. Some of the contributions may in retrospect seem quite simple and obvious: technological innovations can have positive returns, the innovator can fail to appropriate returns unless they possess complementary assets, firms invest in R&D not only to develop new products but to absorb external knowledge and so forth. Yet, these are also enduring and powerful ideas. The question also arises about whether this work would be published in today's environment, where there is an obsession with the *process* of research, that is the purity of methodologies and extent of contributions to theory (both of which are open to subjectivity), rather than its *content*. The lessons for both researchers and the gatekeepers to research publications, particularly journal editors, is that the most enduring and useful research is based not on regimented processes designed to portray some faux scientific respectability, but on the quality of ideas that enlighten and stimulate.

3 Concepts and frameworks

This chapter reviews contributions from researchers that provide insights to help generalize lessons about innovation management. It offers concepts and frameworks that assist understanding of the nature, process and outcomes of innovation management. Innovation is commonly a complex, multi-factored process involving strategies, structures and practices that are idiosyncratic to particular organizations: their markets, cultures and technologies. The insights provided here help make sense of this complexity and assist in the questioning and guiding of approaches to innovation management and provide opportunities for their testing, refutation and development through further research and better empirical evidence.

Defining the amplitude of innovation is one of the most important ways understanding of innovation management is framed. A crucial place to start is differentiating between incremental and radical innovation. Incremental innovations occur in established markets, technologies and ways of doing things close to an organization's existing activities. Radical innovations involve breakthroughs in markets, technologies and ways of doing things very different from those supported by an organization's established resources and capabilities. Between these two levels are those substantial innovations that build upon existing activities, extending and diversifying them into new areas. Incremental innovations involve the renovation of existing products and processes and are the most common form of innovation. Radical innovations are rare, but can be highly consequential.

In their article on "Architectural innovation: the reconfiguration of existing product technologies and the failure of established firms", Rebecca Henderson and Kim Clark (1990) provide further dimensions of innovation's amplitude by discussing *architectural* and *modular innovation*. They distinguish between the components of a product and the ways they are integrated into the system of which they are a part, or their architecture. Using the case of the semiconductor photolithographic alignment equipment industry, they show that minor improvements in technology can subtly alter the product's architecture – that is innovation occurs in architecture while leaving modules or components essentially unchanged. As revealed in a number of case studies, by destroying the embedded organizational and knowledge-based supports for architectures, such architectural innovation poses significant competitive challenges. Henderson and Clark consider the implications of their characterization of innovation for issues such as organizational learning, the organization of cross-functional teams and for competitive strategy.

The notion of *technological discontinuities* has been influential. In their article "Technological discontinuities and organizational environments", Michael Tushman and Philip Anderson (1986) consider the impact of technological breakthroughs on the environments in which firms compete. They study the minicomputer and the cement and airline industries from their birth to 1980, and show that while technology mainly progresses incrementally it experiences intense periods of technological foment and disruption. These technology discontinuities, which sharply improve price-performance relationships, can be *competence-enhancing* or *competence-destroying*. The former tend to emerge within existing firms and build on present knowledge and skills, and the latter from within new firms, requiring new knowledge and skills. Tushman and Anderson explore the implications of technological discontinuities for environmental uncertainty (the extent to which the future can be predicted) and munificence (the extent to which growth is possible). They find the competitive environment is profoundly altered following a technological discontinuity, which provides new opportunities for firms seeking competitive advantage, with implications, for example, for investments in research and development (R&D).

Disruption is ubiquitous in the modern world. Extreme political, economic, environmental, geological and biological events continually introduce new kinds of turbulence for organizations. Innovation is itself a major source of disruption as competitors find ways of doing things better, cheaper and faster. Competitors can increasingly benefit from global access to ideas, production capacities and deregulated markets, and from cheap and ubiquitous digital technologies. As economic systems become ever more complex, interdependent and rapidly changing, the level of disruption that confronts organizations increases. Disruption occurs in business models and cost structures, such as the effect on telecommunications companies of providers of Voice Over Internet Protocol (VOIP) services, or the consequences for high street stores of online shopping. Changes in regulation can be disruptive, such as environmental controls on automobiles, or restrictions on the ability of banks to offer both retail and investment services. The largest challenges emerge when different forms of disruption combine, such as the newspaper industry being confronted by electronic news sources. Technological change is a major source of disruption, especially when new platforms emerge such as new methods of drug discovery by means of genetic engineering. Becoming attuned to potential disruption, and developing the means for dealing with it, are key issues for the management of innovation.

In their article on "Technology brokering and innovation in a product development firm", Andrew Hargadon and Robert Sutton (1997) use an ethnographic study of the leading design company IDEO to discuss the importance of *technology brokering* for the development of innovative products. IDEO is widely recognized for its innovativeness, and the article discusses how it has strong connections in many industries, but is not central to any one, providing the company occasion to learn about many technologies and exploit its network opportunities to combine technologies in ways not seen before. Hargadon and Sutton suggest technology brokering involves more than simply transporting ideas between previously disconnected industries, and sees the – sometimes radical – transformation of ideas into new environments. They offer a process model of innovation involving access, acquisition, storage and retrieval and discuss how IDEO engages with each. The organizational supports for technology brokering include structuring work to give employees breadth of experience, rotation of team membership, incentives for sharing information and careful screening of potential employees. The design methodology and approach adopted by IDEO is argued to have significance for many innovative firms.

Innovation is rarely a solitary phenomenon and invariably involves multiple connections. Ronald Burt (2004) in his article "Structural holes and good ideas" argues that people who stand near the holes in a social structure (where there are no existing connections) are at a higher risk of having good ideas. Opinions and behaviours are more homogenous within groups than between them, and therefore access to disconnected groups (across 'holes') can refresh and stimulate thinking. Burt studies the network connections of 673 managers in the supply chain of one of America's largest electronics companies, an organization full of structural holes. He finds that those managers whose networks span structural holes receive higher compensation, better performance evaluations and more promotions. He also found that such brokers were more likely to express ideas, less likely to have their ideas dismissed, and more likely to have their ideas considered to be valuable. When considering creativity, Burt argues there is a market for the information arbitrage of network entrepreneurs, and that creativity is a diffusion process of repeated discovery across structural holes, with the implication that people should be incentivized to engage with diverse ideas.

One of the factors that limit the flow of information within and between organizations is its 'stickiness'. Eric von Hippel (1994) explores the implications of information that is costly to acquire, transfer and use in his article "'Sticky information' and the locus of problem solving: implications for innovation". He describes four patterns of innovation-related problem solving in *sticky information*. When sticky information is held in one location, innovation problem solving congregates there. When there are multiple loci, problem solving iterates between them. When information is very sticky, tasks can become partitioned into sub-problems. When the costs of iteration are high, investments are made to make information less sticky, for example by making tacit knowledge more codified by capturing it in software or expert systems. Von Hippel discusses the implications of information stickiness for issues such as managing information transfer costs, the protection of intellectual property, and patterns of specialization.

James March's (1991) distinction between *exploration* and *exploitation* is an enduring characterization of the diversity of organizational behaviour. In his paper "Exploration and exploitation in organizational learning", March suggests exploration includes terms such as search, variation, risk, experimentation, play, discovery and innovation. Exploitation, in contrast, is associated with refinement, efficiency, selection, implementation and execution. Organizations that preference exploration to the detriment of exploitation suffer cost blowouts. Organizations that preference exploitation become trapped and unable to change. March's question is how organizations make explicit choices and trade-offs to balance the two. Exploitation involves the refinement and extension of existing competences, and its returns are positive, proximate and predictable. Exploration involves experimentation whose returns are uncertain, distant and often negative. His focus is adaptation and organizational learning. Organizational performance and competitive advantage relies on a delicate trade-off between exploration and exploitation, and March offers insights into the socialization of learning in organizations towards the 'non-trivial' determination of optimality.

Failure is inevitable as organizations innovate. It is usually impossible to predict which new technologies, products and services will succeed. As failure is ubiquitous, it is a crucially important focus of study, and it is, of course, every innovation manager's concern to avoid it where possible. Clayton Christensen's (1997) *The Innovator's Dilemma* asks, "How can great firms fail? Insights from the Hard Disk industry", and offers a framework for understanding the failure of companies. By studying various generations of computer hard disks (14-, 8-, 5.25-, 3.5-, 2.5- and 1.8-inch), he finds that the best firms succeeded in each new generation because they responded to their customers by investing aggressively in technology, products and manufacturing capabilities. And those best firms subsequently failed in the next generation for doing exactly the same thing. Hence his reference to the 'innovator's dilemma'. Christensen distinguishes technologies that *sustain* and those that *disrupt*. Sustaining technologies in hard disks, which were often radical in nature, emerged in established firms. These firms possessed significant technological prowess. Yet it was new entrant firms that led the industry in every instance of generational change. He suggests that leading firms are held captive by their customers, who demand improvements in existing products and technologies in which they have invested, rather than better, disruptive technologies in which they have no position.

Innovations emerge from many sources inside and outside of the innovating organization. One important source is the *user* of innovations. Much of the research on user innovation is associated with Eric von Hippel. In his 1986 article "Lead users: a source of novel product concepts", he argues that *lead users* not only possess strong needs which help innovative firms identify market trends, but they are themselves important sources of innovation. Von Hippel contends that there are considerable limitations when marketing departments ask users for their insights into how markets are developing: users are more comfortable with the familiar than suggesting novel product concepts. His solution is the identification of lead users, who are forward-thinking and can offer valuable insights and even prototype new developments, and he offers guidance on how to recognize them and use them most effectively.

Annabel Gawer and Michael Cusumano (2002) in their book *Platform Leadership* develop the framework of the *platform* or building block which attracts other firms' investment and innovation in add-on products or services. Platform leaders, such as Microsoft Windows or Google, are the centrepiece of evolving ecosystems of separately developed pieces of technology. In the concluding chapter of their book, "The essence of platform leadership", Gawer and Cusumano suggest becoming a platform leader is like finding the Holy Grail: many seek it, but it is found by few. Platforms gain value when used along with 'complements': Intel's semiconductors, for example, depended on developments in the personal computer business. Success as a platform leader depends, therefore, on collaboration with others in developing complementary innovation in platform architecture and interfaces. Using a number of case studies from the information and communications technology industry, Gawer and Cusumano discuss four levers of platform leadership: firms' scope, product technology, external relationships, and internal organization. While platforms are not found in every industry, as a framework for innovation management it is helpful in explaining how leaders in some industries shape its whole development.

The concept of *core capabilities* that differentiate a firm strategically is well entrenched in the management literature, and Dorothy Leonard-Barton (1992) develops an argument about their paradoxical relationship with *core rigidities*. In her article "Core capabilities and core rigidities: a paradox in managing new product development", Leonard-Barton explores how to benefit from capabilities while avoiding their dysfunctional element. She defines a core capability as the knowledge set that distinguishes and provides a competitive advantage. They have four dimensions: employee knowledge and skills, technical and managerial systems, and values and norms associated with knowledge creation and use. By examining 25 cases of new product and process development in five firms, she explores how core capabilities enhance and hinder innovation. Her inclusion of values and norms accentuates how entrenched rigidities can become. She highlights how projects provide opportunities for reflection, learning and change in capabilities, but emphasizes how difficult it is to challenge the construction of capabilities. The most successful strategy involves continuing questioning of their construction and an emphasis on organizational learning.

In another extension of research into the role of capabilities, David Teece, Gary Pisano and Amy Shuen (1997) in their article "Dynamic capabilities and strategic management" analyze the sources and methods of wealth creation and capture by firms experiencing rapid technological change. They see *dynamic capabilities* as a set of differentiated skills, complementary assets and routines that provide the basis for a firm's competitive capacities and sustainable advantage. Their focus on the term 'dynamic' refers to the capacity to renew competences in response to changing environments: the need for innovative responses when speed and timing are critical, where technological change is rapid and the future is uncertain for markets and competition. The term 'capabilities' emphasizes the key role of strategic management in appropriately adapting, integrating and reconfiguring internal and external organizational skills, resources and functional competences to match the needs of a changing environment. Teece and colleagues include an extensive range of components of their framework in processes, positions and paths and their replicability and imitability. They consider the normative implications of their framework for issues such as entry strategies, diversification, focus and specialization. The value of the dynamic capabilities framework lies in its attempt to integrate a range of insights that enfold the complexities of technology-based competitiveness, and it thus stands in stark contrast to the majority of strategic management approaches that fail to do so. It is more a stimulus to thinking than a prescriptive model, and it has spawned a subsequent array of work in the capabilities field that offer none of its insights.

Developing innovative new projects is challenging in large, mature firms, especially those threatened by new technologies, new entrants and changing customer demands. In their article: "Organizing and leading 'heavyweight' development teams", Kim Clark and Steven Wheelwright (1992) suggest a variety of reasons for this, including the tendency towards functional silos that prevent marketing, engineering and manufacturing from communicating effectively with one another. To overcome these problems, Clark and

Wheelwright propose the creation of *heavyweight teams*. They outline four different types of development teams: functional, lightweight, heavyweight and autonomous, and describe the opportunities and challenges of heavyweight teams in comparison to the alternatives. Heavyweight teams have senior leaders who have primary supervisory responsibility for those working in the team, and they are often co-located. Although advantageous in the way they offer better communications, greater commitment and cross-functional coordination, heavyweight teams pose difficulties, requiring changes in individual behaviour and a commitment of the organization to a fundamentally different way of working.

Modesto Maidique (1980) begins his article on "Entrepreneurs, champions, and technological innovation" with a quote from Nobel Prize–winning economist Kenneth Arrow, emphasizing the importance of individual talent in the firm: "There is plenty of reason to suppose that individual talents count for a good deal more than the firm as an organization". Maidique's concern lies with *entrepreneurs* and *champions*, and he examines the different entrepreneurial, managerial and technological roles within the firm and how these roles change as the company grows from a small to an integrated to a diversified organization. He argues that entrepreneurs are essential for radical innovation, but their role depends on the company's stage of development. Such radical innovation requires top management participation to be successful, and as well as the need for product champions, executive champions play an important role, especially in diversified companies. The article uses a literature review and a number of short vignettes to develop a model of the dynamics of the entrepreneur and champion roles. Maidique makes the point that if large organizations are to avoid the rigidity and inertia that accompany their growth, top managers, and especially the CEO, must be personally involved in entrepreneurial networks and provide the resources for innovation and absorb its risks.

Reference is made time and again in the study of innovation management to Schumpeter's insight that innovation involves new combinations. These frequently require the combination of knowledge and resources that reside in different organizations, and their integration involves a process of *collaboration*. This is the focus of the article on "Interorganizational collaboration and the locus of innovation: Networks of learning in biotechnology" by Walter Powell, Kenneth Koput and Laurel Smith-Doerr (1996). They agree that collaboration between firms helps combine complementary assets, but by studying the R&D alliances of a sample of biotechnology firms, they find that in environments of rapidly changing technology where knowledge is broadly distributed, collaboration is not simply a means to compensate for a lack of internal skills, and the locus of innovation lies in the network of inter-organizational relationships. They point to the value in seeing collaborations not as discrete contractual transactions but as evolving strategic relationships, and suggest that being centrally connected in these networks is necessary to achieve valued organizational outcomes. Powell and his colleagues argue that R&D alliances are the admission ticket to the innovation that occurs in inter-organizational networks, and that firms are participating in them more and getting better at learning from them.

Collaboration connects organizations with external parties as they search for, choose and implement innovations. It contributes to an organization's ability to attain complementarities, encourage learning, develop capabilities and deal with uncertainty and complexity (Dodgson, 2014). Collaboration may involve research links with universities and research institutes and collaboration with companies working in similar markets and technologies in various forms of consortia. Connections with customers and suppliers can deliver many benefits for innovation. The capacities to select partners within established value chains and work effectively with them are key management capabilities. The management of innovation additionally involves the ability to search widely for ideas within wider innovation ecosystems, select from them judiciously, manage the potentially increased contest over intellectual property rights, and ensure good information flow and cooperation within the broad network. It is often a challenging process, and managing the inherent instabilities and tensions in collaboration requires careful partner selection and effective structuring and organization.

The *stage gate* framework is one of the most practical tools to emerge to bring discipline to the new product development process. Its creator, Robert Cooper (2005), in his work on "A world class *stage gate®* idea-to-launch framework for your business", contends that when facing increased pressure to reduce the time to develop new products, while improving success rates, firms introduce stage gates to manage, direct and control their innovation initiatives. He describes stage gates as a systematic process – a playbook, game plan or template – for moving a new product process through its various stages from idea to launch, and provides evidence of its efficacy. Firms that use such formal processes are more successful. Ten goals for a successful stage gate framework are outlined in Cooper's book, *Product Leadership*. They include focus, speed, differentiation, cross-functional teams, scalability and performance metrics. The framework itself comprises five stages and gates. The stages follow a discovery and include scoping, building the business case, development, testing and validation, and launch. The gates are essentially stop/go decision points. Key issues arising from the use of such frameworks include how the choice of projects fits within portfolios of product developments and overall product and technology strategies. Other lessons include how to nuance stop/go decisions with opportunities for iteration and search for more information. Organizations commonly have more ideas for innovations than resources to support them, and such stage gate processes bring an objective impartiality that makes decisions less susceptible to organizational rigidities and politics. While numbers of major firms have adopted stage gate processes, some have experienced difficulties with them. A particular concern is a front-end decision about whether the product being developed complements the company's overall strategy. Having the most efficient development processes is of little value if the company is developing the wrong products.

There is considerable debate in the literature on the conditions where it is best to be first to market with an innovation and where it is best to be a follower. Steven Schnaars (1994) contributes to this discussion in his book *Managing Imitation Strategies*, in which he argues the advantages and disadvantages of *imitation*. Schnaars describes the various kinds of imitation, from copies and counterfeits to technological leapfrogging and adaptation to another industry. He makes the point that the best business imitations often combine copying with creativity, adapting products and services to different circumstances. Imitation is not only found in products and services, but also in procedures, processes and strategies. Schnaars brings the question of timing to the fore in innovation management. He argues pioneers bear considerable risks while late entrants miss most of the opportunity. He suggests the early entrant, however, is in a position to earn most of the economic rewards.

One method of rewarding leadership is through intellectual property. Melissa Schilling's (2005) analysis of "Protecting innovation", from her book *Strategic Management of Technological Innovation*, provides a helpful introduction to the *protection* mechanisms that can be used by innovators to appropriate returns from their investments. She discusses the main methods of intellectual property protection: *patents, trademarks* and *copyright*, and the international bodies overseeing their use. She discusses the alternatives, such as trade secrets and rapid diffusion. Schilling discusses the virtues of *open* and *proprietary* systems. The methods and their effectiveness used to protect innovation, she argues, vary considerably both within and across industries. Some industries, such as pharmaceuticals, use legal protections such as patents to great effect. Electronics firms, by contrast, achieve little protection by such methods.

The extent to which pioneers gain distinctive competitive advantage depends, as we have seen in the contribution from Teece on complementary assets, on a variety of conditions. There are, furthermore, a number of ways organizations can derive value from their investments in innovation apart from manifesting them in products and services. Ashish Arora and Alfonso Gambardella (2010) analyze one such path in *markets for technology*. In their article "Ideas for rent: an overview of markets for technology", they argue that technology has become an economic commodity, bought and sold as patents, licenses and other forms of intellectual property, often embedded in technological alliances of some sort. They offer some estimates of the scale of markets for technology, and point to the way that in the Organisation for Economic Co-operation and Development (OECD), growth in technology royalty payments exceeds world gross domestic product (GDP) growth. Arora and Gambardella address the supply and demand of technology, considering among other elements the role of technology specialists versus established firms. They discuss the factors that limit the growth of markets for technology, including uncertainty over intellectual property rights and the implications of markets for technology for industrial structure and their dynamics. Arora and Gambardella's research on markets for technology provides a valuable concept for framing understanding of one broad option for attaining value from innovation.

Basic research, commonly defined as research with no application in mind, is not a concept or framework as such, but a distinctive and important element of innovation in many sectors whose nature and purpose needs to be understood. In his article, Nathan Rosenberg (1990) poses the question: "Why do firms do basic research (with their own money)?" He explains basic research is a long-term investment that firms will only make if they are confident of a rate of return equal to more tangible investments. It is an uncertain investment and its results are often widely available to others and difficult to appropriate. Nevertheless, Rosenberg argues firms can capture significant returns from investments in basic research. These include 'first mover advantages' and consolidating positions in well-established firms with long-term strategies. He discusses basic research in such large firms and in small biotechnology firms. One of Rosenberg's many contributions to the understanding of innovation draws on his background as a historian. By using historical examples, he highlights the common confusions around the boundaries of what is basic and applied research, and he makes the observation that much basic research is undertaken to explain an applied problem such as why a technology works. The high level of interactivity between basic and applied research leads him to think about basic research as an admission ticket to an information network. Rosenberg suggests that the conduct of basic research helps firms make better decisions about where to invest in applied research and to evaluate that research more effectively. It improves firms' monitoring abilities, allowing them to keep abreast of consequential external developments.

One of the major arguments for investments in basic research is the *instrumentation* produced for its conduct. The computer, internet and laser are modern instruments developed for basic research experiments without regard for their commercial application. Derek de Solla Price (1984), in his article "The science/technology relationship, the craft of experimental science, and policy for the improvement of high technology innovation", refers to the importance of 'instrumentalities'. These are instruments and experimental techniques, and Price argues they are crucial means of connecting scientific and technological progress. Using a range of historical examples, from Galileo's use of the telescope to Rosalind Franklin's X-ray diffraction photograph that was vital to Crick and Watson's discovery of DNA, instruments have been crucial contributors to mankind's most fundamental understanding. Price emphasizes the importance not only of instruments, but also processes such as magnetic resonance imaging and laboratory methods for organizing experiments and data. The changes in experimental methods brought about by online tools and big data will undoubtedly induce a new era where Price's instrumentalities assume a continuing, and perhaps even greater, centrality (Nielsen, 2012). New processes such as CRISPR, a genome editing tool, can radically transform innovation in fields as broad as biology and bioengineering. Artificial intelligence (AI) is being used to develop scientific hypotheses and significantly increase the speed and pre-dictability of experimentation. Of all the future developments in the field of innovation management, the impact of new digital technologies on the design, development and diffusion of innovations is likely to be the most significant.

4   Important empirical studies

This chapter considers research on innovation management because of the particular *strength* or *novelty* of their empiricism or because they are revealing of a particular empirical *method*. Many could also be included in other chapters on the strength of the insights they develop. Similarly, many of the contributions on foundations, concepts and frameworks of innovation management are empirically based and could be included here. Their allocation is somewhat subjective, but each paper discussed in this chapter makes a valuable empirical contribution.

The study of innovation management uses a broad range of quantitative and qualitative research methods, covers a wide span, including nations, industries, sectors and different sizes of organizations, and explores an extensive number of issues. Studies include sophisticated econometric analysis of large databases on the one hand, and cases of individual companies and innovators on the other. There are considerable methodological difficulties in studying innovation empirically. Cause and effect are difficult to determine; correlation does not imply causation (does research and development [R&D] lead to high profits, or do high profits encourage R&D?); time is a crucial factor, so over what period of time should outcomes such as success be assessed?; and given the diversity in levels and types of innovation, what is actually being measured?

One of the major issues and difficulties with empirical studies of innovation lies in the measures being used. Patents are commonly used, but these are only a proxy measure of innovation and are of particular relevance in a relatively limited number of industries. As argued in the previous chapter, Melissa Schilling shows the pharmaceutical industry uses patents to great effect, while electronics firms achieve little protection from them. Studies use patents as an input to and output of the innovation process. R&D expenditure and intensity are regularly used measures, but there remain definitional difficulties and also these data may fail to capture investments made by smaller firms. At the extreme polarity of 'R' can be some fundamental research with very long-term horizons and no concept of market application; at the other polarity of 'D' can be some very minor incremental improvements. Yet companies positioned at either extremity are judged to be undertaking 'R&D'. Other studies use existing innovation databases, recorded, for example, in trade journals or as award winners, or construct their own measures of innovativeness by examining particular innovations.

Project SAPPHO is in many ways the foundational empirical study of innovation. It undertook a comparative analysis of 'paired' *successful* and *unsuccessful* technological innovations – half successful, half unsuccessful in having obtained a worthwhile market share and profit – and examined the factors determining these different outcomes. "SAPPHO updated – project SAPPHO phase II", by Roy Rothwell, Christopher Freeman, A. Horlsey, V. Jervis, A. Robertson and Joe Townsend (1974), reports on two studies. The first phase of this study examined 29 pairs: 17 in chemical processes and 12 in scientific instruments. Using 122 measures, it found differences in success was explained by understanding user needs, efficiency of development processes, characteristics of managers, efficiency of communications, and marketing and sales efforts. The second phase extended to include 43 pairs: 22 in chemical processes and 21 in scientific instruments. This confirmed the findings of Phase 1, but accentuated sectoral differences especially related to underlying environmental and structure differences in the two industries. So, for example, in the scientific instruments industry, what mattered more was the experience and commitment of the innovator rather than the formal status and degree of power found in chemicals. The 34 failure cases were examined in more detail and additional factors were explored, such as investments in basic research, speed to market and degree of innovativeness. In summary, Project SAPPHO found success in innovation lay with user needs being precisely determined and met, and good communications and integration across the organization from R&D to production to marketing. It found various management techniques were of value, but these were no substitution for managers of high quality and ability. SAPPHO found that success cannot be explained by single factors: innovation involves many and diverse contributors.

Edward Mansfield (1991) was one of the first to explore the connection between *academic research* and innovation. In "Academic research and industrial innovation", he estimated the extent to which technological innovations were based on recent academic research, the time lags between research and its industrial application, and the social returns from academic research. Mansfield selected a random sample of 76 major American firms in seven manufacturing industries. He researched the proportion of the firms' new products and processes commercialized over a ten-year period that could have not have been developed without substantial delay in the absence of academic research undertaken within 15 years of that innovation's introduction. He found that 11 per cent of firms' new products and 9 per cent of their new processes could not have been introduced without such academic input. The more R&D-intensive industries had higher connections with academic research. Mansfield estimated that 3 per cent of the total sales of the sample firms resulted from product innovations reliant on academic research, which was also responsible for a 1 per cent saving in total costs through process innovation. The mean time lag in the transfer from research to innovation was 7 years. While accepting his measures are crude, Mansfield tentatively estimated a social rate of return from academic research of 28 per cent. He shows that some industries, such as pharmaceuticals, scientific instruments and information processing, have much higher reliance on academic research. He concludes that research has many benefits beyond industrial innovation alone, but even using this metric, its contribution is substantial.

Assessing the extent to which investments in science pay off has been a challenging empirical problem. Michael Gibbons and Ron Johnston (1974) in "The role of science in technological innovation" suggest that the *returns to science* are complex and often indirect. They argue science contributes to innovation in many ways apart from the direct application of discoveries, and include the valuable interpersonal networks that are created between people working in research and business and are important means for solving problems. They also suggest that it is a mistake to consider this relationship only in major, radical innovations, and it is also important to assess science's contributions to the small incremental changes that are cumulatively so important. Gibbons and Johnson studied 30 innovations in depth, researching their sources and the impact of those sources. They find university research is valuable in the scientific knowledge it produces, making the important and still very contemporary observation that a key element of industry-university interfaces is industry's recognition of the contribution of fundamental rather than applied research. They also highlight the importance of the educational levels of 'problem solvers', showing those with university educations are more likely to search widely for solutions to problems. Gibbons and Johnston conclude that because of the complexity of the relationship between science and innovation, it is very difficult to estimate an optimum level of investment in science. It is, however, important to continue to understand the multiple ways innovation relates to science.

Richard Rosenbloom and Michael Cusumano (1987) analyze the question of *technological leadership* and competitive advantage. In their research on "Technological pioneering and competitive advantage: the birth of the VCR industry", they undertake six company case studies: RCA, Ampex, JVC, Matsushita, Toshiba and Sony. The changing dynamics of leadership is explored in the cases, showing whereas much of the early technological advantage in videocassette recorders lay with the American companies, the winners in the market were the Japanese firms. Their success lay with their focus on the most rewarding opportunities, better positioning of their technical efforts and more adept engagement of all the constituents in the evolving market. They emphasize the winners' strategic clarity, consistency and learning ability and the considerable rewards that derive from being a pioneer. Rosenbloom and Cusumano also point to how limited is the window of opportunity to enter new and complex technologies. The Japanese firms succeeded, not because they had any distinctive national advantage, but because they had very effective management practices based around strategic experimentation and disciplined learning.

The relative advantage of *large* and *small* firms in innovation continues to be an important issue, the basic premise being that firms differ in what and how they innovate according to their size. Rothwell and Dodgson (1994), for example, distinguish the resource and material advantages (investments in R&D, production and distribution) of the large firm from the behavioural advantages (speed of response, flexibility) of the small firm, explaining in part the virtues of collaboration between them. One of the earliest contributions to this discussion is "Innovation in large and small firms: an empirical analysis" by Zoltan Acs and David Audretsch (1988). These researchers use a database of innovations collected by the US Small Business Administration, in which innovations were allocated into industry of origin and it was determined whether they emerged in large firms (more than 500 employees) or small firms (fewer than 500 employees). (It is to be noted here that this definition of a small firm differs from many, which commonly define a small firm as one with fewer than 200 employees). There appeared to be no difference in the 'quality' or novelty of the innovations between large and small firms. Whereas large firm innovations exceeded small firm innovations in 21 of the 35 most innovative industries, the reverse was the case in 14 industries. A correlation was found between this innovation measure and R&D expenditure: the number of innovations increases with increased industry R&D expenditures, but at a decreasing rate. The more concentrated the industry, the lower its innovativeness. Acs and Audretsch point to the limitations of their data and its analysis, but suggest it provides support for the argument that large and small firms innovate in different technological and economic environments.

Ove Granstrand and Sören Sjölander (1990) introduce the concept of the *multi-technology* corporation. Defined as a company working in more than three technologies, these authors use case studies of Ericsson and Saab-Scania and then explore the significance of their concept in a wider sample of Sweden's 24 largest R&D spenders. Ericsson is used as an example of a company transforming its technology base (from electro-mechanical to digital switches). Saab-Scania is used as an example of a company transferring technology among business units. Granstrand and Sjölander outline the context in which multi-technology corporations are growing in importance. They suggest a key focus of technology strategy is the technology base, or capability, of the company, and consider the technology acquisition strategies that supplement the base and the technology exploitation strategies that draw on it. Ericsson's challenge was to substitute technologies in the base; Saab-Scania's was how to organize internal technology transfer to reap synergies. The authors identify a number of critical management abilities for these two generic situations.

The question of how *large* firms are entrepreneurial is the basis of Gautam Ahuja and Curba Lampert's (2001) work on "Entrepreneurship in the large corporation: a longitudinal study of how established firms create breakthrough inventions". They argue large firms suffer three innovation-stifling pathologies – favouring the familiar, the mature and the propinquitous – and argue that experimenting with novel, emerging and pioneering technologies can help firms overcome these traps and create breakthrough innovations. Novel technologies are those with which the firm lacks prior experience; emerging technologies are recently developed in the industry; and pioneering technologies do not build upon existing technologies. Their empirical study is based on a longitudinal data set on the patenting activities of the global chemical industry over a 15-year period. They identify breakthrough inventions as being in the top 1 per cent of the most cited patents. Ahuja and

Lampert find a curvilinear relationship between exploration of novel and emerging technologies and subsequent breakthrough inventions, however the downward part of the slope was not identifiable in the case of pioneering technologies. They argue that large firm tendencies towards the familiar, mature and propinquitous are not dysfunctional or inept, but are efficient responses to the circumstances of the firm. They are not, however, helpful if the firm wishes to develop breakthrough inventions, which instead require entrepreneurship encouraging of diversity and experimentation to overcome the learning traps that accompany organizational maturity and size.

3M is near the top of the list of the world's most consistently innovative large firms. In their article on "Innovative science and technology commercialization strategies at 3M: a case study", Pedro Conceição, Dennis Hamill and Pedro Pinheiro (2002) begin by describing the constraints to innovation in large companies and the strategies 3M uses to overcome them. They describe 3M's general policies and culture supporting innovation, and then examine a case within a case of one particular group in electronics and its strategies for coordinating innovation across its various businesses. The authors discuss the many practices 3M has in place encouraging innovation in the company's strategy, culture and environment, networks, organization form, and motivations and incentives. Conceição and colleagues use the case of a new electronics initiative to reveal how 3M is open to new ways of organizing. Its divisional organizational structure, which had been very successful in the past, was inappropriate for the opportunities provided by electronics, which crossed 14 divisions. The new structure created to coordinate innovations across the company reflected 3M's concern to maintain innovation leadership through exploring new organizational forms.

As noted in the case of 3M, a company's leadership and culture for innovation are crucially important assets. Being prepared for an uncertain future is deeply dependent on leadership and culture. Culture shapes the degree to which an organization looks forward or focuses on the past, and also determines the rate of change and innovation that organizational members are comfortable dealing with. Leadership plays a similarly central role in the degree to which an organization is future ready. If leaders are forward-looking and provide the sort of transformational leadership that makes organizational members feel secure and empowered, then awareness of the need to change, ideas for innovation and a willingness to change to meet future challenges will all increase. Supportive leadership and cultures are seen in tolerance of risk and change and in the support provided for creativity. One concept used to analyze adventurous, flexible and responsive behaviours is the notion of play (Dodgson, Gann and Salter, 2005). Play at work encompasses those activities where people experiment, explore, template, model, prototype, rehearse and tinker with new ideas, often in combination with others with different skills in stimulating environments where work rules are relaxed. Play, in this sense, is an antidote to the procedures and bureaucracy that inevitably develops in organizations over time, and are anathema to innovation.

Xerox is another company atop many observers' lists of the world's most innovative companies, with especial consideration of its Palo Alto Research Centre (PARC). Henry Chesbrough and Richard Rosenbloom (2002) explore "The role of the business model in capturing value from innovation: evidence from Xerox Corporation's technology spin-off companies". They bring to the fore the concept of the *business model*, a focusing device which connects technical potential with economic value creation. The inherent value in a technology remains latent, they contend, until it is commercialized using a business model that may or may not be already familiar to the firm. The paper describes how the Haloid Corporation (which became Xerox) attempted to attract leading corporates, such as Kodak, GE and IBM, into partnerships to develop its photocopying technology. These partners were not attracted because they saw the value of the technology through the limited lens of the existing business model. When Xerox developed the idea of its novel business model of leasing and payments above a number of copies, the value of the technology was realized to an extraordinary degree. Chesbrough and Rosenbloom argue that this business model became embedded in Xerox's thinking, with some successes and many limitations. The paper examines six spin-offs from PARC; one succeeded and two failed using Xerox's existing business model, three succeeded only after using a substantially different business model. The successful business models emerged following close engagement with customers. The authors conclude that technology managers cannot disregard concern for the business models that are responsible for the creation of value.

One of the most critical mistakes innovation management researchers and practitioners can make is to assume that everything is new under the sun. There is much to learn from the past, and the ways that problems were addressed and resolved in history hold many lessons for the present and future. As Stephen Barley (1998) has pointed out, historical analyses also have the virtue of being enacted: we know what happened. "When

innovations meet institutions: Edison and the design of the electric light"
by Andrew Hargadon and Yellowlees Douglas (2001) is an exemplary
demonstration of drawing on the past to illuminate the present. Their work
considers the central role of *design* as the emergent arrangement of con-
crete details that embodies a new idea, in mediating between innovations
and established institutional fields. The case study used is Edison's system
of electric lighting. The authors argue that Edison triumphed over the gas
lighting industry by cloaking his radical innovation in the mantle of existing institutions and what was familiar to consumers. Edison's challenge
was immense. Gas companies were well established and woven into New
York's physical infrastructure and institutions. There was scientific scepti-
cism about the feasibility of electric lighting, and entrenched obstacles in,
for example, regulations that only allowed gas companies to dig up streets
to lay pipes. Gas companies reduced their prices considerably to see off the
opposition. Edison mirrored existing institutions as much as possible, such
as in localized generation, and retrofitted house fittings such as gas lamps to
electricity so as not to be too unfamiliar to users. Hargadon and Yellowlees
use the concept of robust designs (see also Gardiner and Rothwell, 1988) to
explain Edison's successful approach and also consider its application in a
number of contemporary innovations.

Josiah Wedgwood was one of history's greatest innovators, and in Mark
Dodgson's article, "Exploring new combinations in innovation and entrepreneurship: social networks, Schumpeter, and the case of Josiah Wedgwood (1730–1795)", he brings consideration of *social networks* into
Schumpeterian analysis of *entrepreneurship*. Building on the importance of
'new combinations', and by using secondary and primary historical sources,
he explores the extensive range of Wedgwood's innovations in products,
processes, markets, supply and organization. Dodgson analyzes the broad
range of social networks – family, economic and patronage – that Wedgwood utilized in his innovations, and argues the value of both strong and
weak ties in his networks. The article argues that his networks added to both
his technological and market innovations. Wedgwood's case tells us about
more than the considerable business advantages of new combinations, and
in the context of the turmoil of the Industrial Revolution is revealing of the
wider economic benefits of combining business and science, and artists and
industrial design, which remain of considerable contemporary significance.

The structures of *networks* that support innovation have been the focus
of extensive research interest. Gautam Ahuja (2000) in "Collaborative

networks, structural holes, and innovation: a longitudinal study" develops a theoretical framework for a firm's 'ego' network, and explores it empirically using patent and collaboration data in the chemical industry. He distinguishes direct ties, indirect ties and structural holes (where there are no connections). The paper begins with a discussion of the divergent views in the literature about the benefits and disadvantages of different network structures. Ahuja then examines firms' network position in the chemical industry and their relationship with its patenting performance (as a measure of innovation). He found that direct and indirect ties positively influence innovation, but the impact of indirect ties is impacted by the firm's level of direct ties. He also found in his study that increasing structural holes decreases innovation output. Ahuja considers the normative implications of his study, and concludes that much depends on the benefits being sought from networks and there is no simple, universal answer to the most effective network structures.

Ray Reagans and Bill McEvily (2003) in "Network structure and knowledge transfer: the effects of cohesion and range" show a similar concern with the structure of networks, but they use a very different research method. Theirs is the study of a contract research company, and their focus is on how *network* structure influences the *knowledge transfer* process. They argue that social cohesion, that is one surrounded by strong third-party connections, around a relationship encourages individuals to contribute to knowledge sharing and that the range of network connections – with ties to different knowledge pools – increases a person's ability to convey complex information to diverse audiences. These two factors – social cohesion and range – ease knowledge transfer over and above the strength of the tie between two people. Reagans and McEvily's methods involved administering a survey instrument in the company over two days, and information gleaned from the person in the company responsible for knowledge management and from the human resources department. They contribute to the discussion in the literature about the value of strong ties for the transfer of tacit knowledge, and argue the optimum network structure combines elements of cohesion and range.

The value of analogies is shown particularly clearly in Hirotaka Takeuchi and Ikujiro Nonaka's (1986) article on "The new product development game". They argue the value in thinking about *new product development* not as a relay race, with one function handing over to another in a linear progression, but a game of rugby, with different functions inter-lapped and interlaced. Their study includes a comparison of the traditional sequential product development process found at NASA, with the more holistic approach found in Japanese companies such as Fuji-Xerox, Canon, Honda and NEC. The researchers particularly studied the development processes in six specific products in these Japanese companies. The holistic approach they found encompasses built-in instability, self-organizing project teams, 'multilearning' across different organizational levels and functions, subtle control and the organizational transfer of learning. Takeuchi and Nonaka argue that in fast-paced, highly competitive environments where speed and flexibility are at a premium, the holistic, rugby-like process brings many benefits. They also suggest that the new approach to the product development process has the capacity to change the rest of the organization, challenging rigidities by introducing new creative, market-driven ideas.

The organization of R&D teams is a central concern for the study of innovation management. In "Project performance and the locus of influence in the R&D matrix", Ralph Katz and Tom Allen (1985) study the relationship between project performance and the relative influence of project and functional managers. Their study is of 86 R&D teams in nine technology-based organizations. The *R&D matrix* form of organization emerged to address the problems of functional managers, whose departments are organized along disciplines or technologies, struggling to coordinate interdisciplinary projects, and those of project managers, whose responsibilities focus on a problem or project, being unable to keep pace with technical developments in the disciplines. In matrix organization there are three broad areas where both project and functional managers are supposed to be involved: technical decisions, determination of salaries and promotions, and staffing and organizational assignments. Katz and Allen studied these activities by surveying 486 engineers in 86 projects, and studied the performance of the teams by a number of criteria adjudged by numbers of more senior managers. They found that for good performance the project manager should be concerned with external relations, obtaining resources and liaising with marketing and manufacturing. Functional managers should be inward-looking, focusing chiefly on the technology that goes into the project. The authors acknowledge the roles can never be separate and that matrix organization is challenging, and point to the importance of strong working relationships between project and functional managers.

"Resolving the capability-rigidity paradox in new product innovation" by Kwaku Atuahene-Gima (2005) provides an early example of a survey questionnaire conducted in China. An interviewer scheduled appointments with two key informants in each firm, presented the questionnaire to them, and then collected them on completion. A total of 227 questionnaires was collected from a sample of 500. The questionnaire was translated from English into Chinese and then reverse translated to check accuracy. The study was designed to resolve the familiar *capability-rigidity* tension analyzed by Leonard-Barton (see Chapter 1). The author suggests that a 'market orientation' resolves the tension, and focusing on customers and competitors ensures simultaneous investments in exploiting existing product innovation competencies and exploring new ones.

The importance of corporate *culture* is explored in "Radical innovation across nations: the pre-eminence of corporate culture" by Gerard Tellis, Jaideep Prabhu and Rajesh Chandy (2009). They contend that radical innovation is a major driver of corporate success and the wealth of nations, and that it is supported by capital, labour, government policies and corporate culture. They examine corporate culture by studying the core set of attitudes and practices shared by members of the firm. Attitudes include willingness to cannibalize assets, future orientation and tolerance of risk. Practices include empowerment of product champions, incentives for enterprise and the creation of internal markets. They measured radical innovation and financial performance. The researchers undertook a survey in 17 nations – the world's eight largest countries, four that have rapidly developed, and five with major innovative or multinational firms – and constructed a sample size of 759 firms. Their quantitative analysis found the effects of future market orientation, willingness to cannibalize and tolerance for risk to be particularly strong influences on performance. R&D was found to be influential, but patenting was not. Tellis, Prabhu and Chandy conclude that corporate culture is a factor that is unique, intangible, sticky and difficult to change, and as the other conditions that affect innovation – capital, labour and government policies – become more unified as globalization increases, corporate culture becomes ever more important as a determinant of the radical innovations that underlie financial performance.

One of the areas to have received relatively little attention in the innovation management literature is the effect of *mergers and acquisitions* (M&A) on innovation. One exception is Gautam Ahuja and Riitta Katila's (2001) "Technological acquisitions and the innovation performance of acquiring firms: a longitudinal study". Theirs is a study of 72 leading companies from the global chemical industry and their acquisition behaviour over a 12-year period, examining the impact of acquisitions on the patenting frequency of the acquiring firm. They distinguish between technological acquisitions, acquisitions in which technology is a component of the acquired firm's assets, and acquisitions that do not involve a technological component. They assess the absolute size, relative size and relatedness of the acquisition. Ahuja and Katila find non-technological acquisitions have no effect on subsequent innovation (measured by patenting). Absolute size of the acquired knowledge base has a positive effect on innovation output, while relative size reduces innovative output. The relatedness of acquired knowledge has a curvilinear relationship with patenting, with high and low levels of relatedness being inferior to moderate levels of relatedness.

Technical standards are an important issue for innovation management in a number of industries, and are the focus of Aija Leiponen's (2008) study "Competing through cooperation: the organization of standard setting in wireless communications". Her research examines the cooperative creation of compatibility standards in wireless communications, focusing on the roles of the standards body and industry consortia and private alliances. She describes how standards are formal or informal agreements and can have dramatic repercussions for firm performance, competition and industry development, because they can lock markets into specific, often partially proprietorial, standards for long periods. Her study examines one of the third generation wireless telecommunications standards, coordinated by 3GPP, and she researches the formal standardization processes in 3GPP and the consortia and alliances that participating firms have outside of the standards body. She studies the work of the standards committee in approving and changing standards, and collects data on participating firms' patenting performance and alliance and consortium memberships. Leiponen finds that participation in external consortia is an important determinant of the ability to create and change standards, and argues the importance of connections as political capital. She contends that her results emphasize the importance of a multipronged cooperation strategy, and how this proves daunting to smaller firms lacking resources.

In "Innovation management measurement: a review", Richard Adams, John Bessant and Robert Phelps (2006) develop a synthesized framework of the innovation management process. It offers a framework for analyzing a wide variety of *measurements* of innovation management, and therefore provides one means of being able to categorize various empirical studies. Their particular framework offers seven categories: inputs management, knowledge management, innovation strategy, organizational culture and structure, portfolio management, project management and commercialization. They then review research publications under each category. Theirs is an initial and helpful attempt at such a review, and the fact that the literature they review is partial and there are many other ways of categorizing reveals the scale and richness of the field of innovation management.

Innovation studies are fortunate nowadays to have access to the power of social networking analysis (SNA) as a new method for studying innovation management. As discussed by Kastelle and Steen (2014), by mapping connections between people, groups, and organizations SNA provides one of the best tools for innovation managers. Kastelle and Steen show how new statistical methods that examine large networks and test hypotheses about network structures and dynamics have dramatically changed the theories and techniques of network analysis, and they provide a guide on how to conduct an analysis. They outline some of the benefits of SNA for innovation managers, which include the identification of organizational silos, finding hubs and key actors, locating isolated people and groups, and identifying bottlenecks.

The most powerful empirical studies are often those that utilize more than one research method. These may combine quantitative and qualitative research, or contemporary and historical data. Although these can be difficult to achieve, they are to be encouraged for the confidence they engender in their findings. At the very least, quality empirical work clearly explains the shortcomings in the research methods chosen.

5   Current and emerging themes

This chapter focuses on a wide range of issues that are of particular contemporary interest. Some of the issues discussed are completely new and previously did not arise or exist, for example novel approaches to innovation enabled by new digital technologies. Others have been rediscovered, refreshed and repackaged, and build upon the robust findings of the past. Others offer fresh new insights into the management of contemporary innovation issues in, for example the environment, projects or engagement of innovators in emerging economies. Each study reported says something of significance for the modern-day study of innovation management.

Roberti Verganti (2008) offers a novel insight into the nature of *design-driven* innovation in his article "Design, meanings, and radical innovation: a metamodel and a research agenda". He contrasts user-centred design, which is used by designers to better understand users and their needs, with design-driven innovation. The latter changes the emotional and symbolic content of products, and their meanings for users, by a deep understanding of the broader changes occurring in technology, society and culture. He uses the example of the Alessi company, which designs eccentric and colourful kitchen appliances, and moved a product category from the staid and functional to the playful and fun. Verganti develops a metamodel that explains the basic mechanisms underlying design-driven innovation, and considers how this model links with existing approaches to innovation management. The metamodel includes a manufacturer's 'interpreters' of the changing world, such as architects, artists, the media and firms in other industries. Verganti admits that there is much work still to be done in improving understanding of design-driven innovation, and he proposes a future research agenda.

The concept of *business models* is an increasing focus of research attention. There is much confusion over what business models are, and how they differ from business strategies. In their article "Clarifying business models: origins, present, and future of the concept", Alexander Osterwalder, Yves Pigneur and Chris Tucci (2005) refer to how their survey of 62 people on what they took to mean by business models elicited 54 different definitions. Their article clarifies the concept of business models and its use in one domain: information systems. In their view, business models are essentially a conceptual tool expressing the business logic of a firm and how it delivers value to itself and its customers. Their article discusses the various components and levels of business model, and five categories of its use: understanding and sharing, analyzing, managing, prospects and patenting. They argue that while the concept still needs further development, it is of considerable use, especially in information systems.

The issue of *services* innovation is one that has a relatively long history and a long history of relative neglect when considering the significance of services compared to the much more frequently studied manufacturing sector. Tether (2014) explains the differences of innovation in services, including their intangible and perishable nature. He shows how it is typified by frequent involvement by users and providers of complementary services, is less reliant on specific departments, such as research and development (R&D), and is more distributed with many diverse contributors. Many service innovations, he argues, involve business model innovation, and he offers a framework of stages and associated tools for services design. Wilfred Dolfsma (2004), in his article "The process of new service development – issues of formalization and appropriability", identifies why services innovations are relatively neglected and what needs to be done to improve their conduct and study. He suggests services innovation tends to be *ad hoc*, and explains this is related to the nature of services being intangible, being co-produced between firm and customer, perishable and 'experienced'. He addresses the difficulty of selecting projects when innovation is *ad hoc*, and the challenges of quality control, standardization and appropriability. Dolfsma argues the need for formalization of new services development and how it improves chances of success, and how involvement of different functions and agents inside and outside of the firm need to be implicated in services innovation. He contends there is much firms can do to improve the process by which they innovate new services.

Decisions about innovation inevitably involve issues of finance. Although this is a perennial issue, its critical continuing importance is seen in the impact of the 2008/9 financial crisis for the declining availability of finance for innovation. Whether it is concerned with levels and quality of venture capital, or the capacity of firms to raise capital in markets or invest retained earnings, the availability of finance is essential for innovation. Hughes (2014) places the issue of innovation funding within the broader context of national governance of capital markets and financial systems. He shows the considerable international variation in the balance of public and private funding of R&D, and draws on analysis of varieties of capitalism and systems of innovation to identify trends in financing.

Innovation is found in all sectors and elements of the economy, including large infrastructural *projects*. Andrew Davies, David Gann and Tony Douglas (2009), in their article "Innovation in megaprojects: systems integration at London Heathrow Terminal 5", provide an example of how innovation addressed many of the challenges of such projects, which are notorious for cost overruns and delays. The project was very large and complex, and using traditional approaches to its construction would not have delivered the requirements of its owner. The authors develop a model of innovation in projects, which are by definition unique, and identify some of the key aspects of the new approach adopted at Terminal 5. These include high levels of systems integration and novel project and program management. Techniques such as single-model digital environments, modular pre-assemblies and just-in-time delivery were used. While these techniques were well used in other sectors, much of the innovation in Terminal 5 lay in their use for the first time in the construction sector. The authors identify the importance of strong leadership with coherent vision and organizational change programmes to support the new behaviours required. The approach to innovation developed during the Terminal 5 project has been used in subsequent major projects in the UK, such as the London Olympics (Davies and Mackenzie, 2013) and Crossrail, the new railway line crossing London (Dodgson, Gann, MacAulay and Davies, 2015).

As one of the pressing issues of the age, *climate change* and *sustainability* more generally is of great concern for innovation management. Innovations are being explored to mitigate the consequences of technologies and products that cause environmental damage and which develop 'clean and green' alternatives. Frans Berkhout, Julia Hertin and David Gann (2006) address the capacity of organizations to adapt in their article "Learning to adapt: organizational adaptation to climate change impacts". Drawing on the organizational learning and innovation literatures, the authors argue that business organizations face a number of obstacles to their learning how to adapt to climate change impacts. They point to the confusion caused by ambiguity of signals about climate change and uncertainty about the benefits to be derived from adaptation measures. Organizational responses are strongly affected by government policy, market conditions and external resources. The article examines processes of adaptation in nine companies in two sectors in the UK, exploring how those firms perceive, interpret and respond to climate change. The authors suggest there are four modes of adaptation: commercial, technological, financial and information and monitoring. They identify four alternative adaptation strategies: wait and see, risk assessment and options appraisal, bearing and managing risks, and sharing and shifting risks.

Berkhout (2014) outlines why environmental sustainability has become such a crucial innovation management concern. He identifies three main influences of technology on business environmental performance: sensing and providing information, improving efficiencies, and transforming resource-use and environmental impacts. He argues that because of the systemic complexities of environmental challenges, responses need to be transformative, requiring a mixture of old and new innovation capabilities, new business models, and linkages.

Previous chapters have discussed the importance of *users* for innovation, and Eric von Hippel (2005), in the chapter "Innovation communities" in his book *Democratizing Innovation*, analyzes how users combine with innovators and with themselves to produce better outcomes. He shows how innovation communities often use collaborative tools and infrastructure that increase the speed and effectiveness by which innovators can develop, test and diffuse their innovations. One of the advantages of innovation communities is their diversity: they bring different knowledge bases and perspectives to bear. Innovation communities can be specialized in membership and focus or can draw on people from outside their usual boundaries. They are based on the preparedness of innovators to reveal information which users find interesting. Von Hippel uses the cases of open source software and the development of the sport of kitesurfing as examples of the nature and contribution of user communities. He makes the point that these communities not only connect innovators with users, but also connect users to other users.

Lars Bo Jeppesen and Lars Frederiksen (2006) provide an in-depth study of a *user community* in their paper "Why do users contribute to firm-hosted user communities? The case of computer-controlled music instruments". They study Propellerhead, a small Swedish company producing software tools for music production, processing and recording. Propellerhead put one of its prototypes on the Web to monitor the potential of the product. The first day, it received 30 hits, the next 3,000, and thereafter 30,000 hits a day. Using interviews, internet questionnaires and weblogs, the authors ask the question of why such users contribute to firm-hosted user communities. They find innovative users are hobbyists (rather than professionals working in the industry), keen to share innovations, who appreciate the firm hosting the community and want to be recognized by it. Users benefit from the improved products they use and firms benefit from being able to improve their products and increase sales. Firms benefit particularly because those contributing tend to be leading-edge users, capable of delivering important, high-quality innovations.

One of the most popular concepts to emerge in innovation management in the twenty-first century is that of *open* innovation. Building on an existing base of knowledge about innovation management going back to Project SAPPHO (see Chapter 4), open innovation contends companies have choices in the way they can bring external connections into their development processes and in the way they get innovations to market. In the introduction to his 2003 book *Open Innovation*, Henry Chesbrough, the researcher who popularized the concept of open innovation, contrasts the declining fortunes of Lucent, heir to the huge scientific strengths of Bell Labs, and successes of Cisco, that did little R&D itself. He suggests this is revealing of a shift in innovation paradigms from closed to open. Closed innovation assumes principles such as the importance of discovery and being first to market. Open innovation assumes firms do not need to originate the research to benefit from it, and better business models are more effective than being first to market. Open innovation assumes firms use external as well as internal ideas, and internal and external paths to market, to further their innovations. The causes of the shift in paradigm include the growing mobility of highly experienced and skilled people, growth of venture capital supporting start-ups, increased need for speed to market of innovations, and growth in the number of knowledgeable customers and international competitors.

Chesbrough's book excited a large number of studies, and one of the best empirically based studies is Keld Laursen and Ammon Salter's (2006) article "Open for innovation: the role of openness in explaining innovation performance among UK manufacturing firms". The paper has a sample of 2,707 firms from the UK innovation survey. The authors are concerned with how firms *search* externally for innovation and determine measures of external search breadth and depth. They find searching widely and deeply across a variety of channels helps firms find and exploit innovation opportunities. They also find that search is not costless, and some firms are capable of 'over-search'. They determine a curvilinear (inverted U) relationship between innovative performance and depth of search: firms can search too little and too much; that is, firms can be too open. Among the many valuable findings in the paper is the substitutional relationship between external search activities and internal R&D.

Another attempt to refine the concept of open innovation is provided by Linus Dahlander and David Gann (2010) in their paper "How open is innovation?" These authors undertake a bibliographic analysis of the open innovation literature with a systematic content analysis. Their review suggests a number of different elements to open innovation, identifying two inbound processes (*sourcing* and *acquiring*) and two outbound processes (*revealing* and *selling*). These processes differ in whether they involve financial exchanges. Revealing and sourcing are non-pecuniary and deliver indirect benefits to the firm; selling and acquiring are pecuniary. By outlining these differences, the authors point to shortcomings in the open innovation literature that assume a more unified concept. They consider the implications of their research for management practice.

The ability of firms to be open in their innovation processes depends to a significant extent on the *technology* that facilitates their external connections. This is the argument presented by Mark Dodgson, David Gann and Ammon Salter (2006) in their study of "The role of technology in the shift towards open innovation: the case of Procter & Gamble". This company is in many ways the poster child of open innovation, with a number of studies of its change in strategy that made it more receptive to external connections, particularly its 'Connect and Develop' strategy. This particular study explores the technological underpinning of openness at Procter & Gamble (P&G). The technologies extend beyond information and communications technology that allow the exchange of distributed sources of information in open innovation. They include a new collection of technologies for data mining, simulation, prototyping and visual representation, which the authors collectively call 'innovation technology' (Dodgson, Gann and Salter, 2005). The authors identify the importance of this enabling technology, but also point to how the changes associated with the move to open innovation at

P&G have built on a number of structural and cultural changes experienced in the company over many years.

The importance of technology used for innovation is further explored in " 'In case of fire, please use the elevator': simulation technology and organization in fire engineering" by Mark Dodgson, David Gann and Ammon Salter (2007). This paper explores the emergence of the new organizational field of fire engineering. The study is framed in the context of the nature of *engineering knowledge* and *boundary objects*. Building on a case study of the engineering company, Arup, it examines the process by which a radical innovation emerged (using lifts for egress from tall buildings in extreme events) and how a number of technologies used as a boundary object helped resolve tensions among multiple, diverse and discordant actors striving for a shared appreciation of negotiated futures. The authors identify a number of internal, integrative and collective intermediary processes associated with the use of the technology: constructing judgment, brokering, forming new combinations, cautious validating, shared imagining and creating the institutional field. Many innovation researchers refer to the importance of experimentation, and these new digital technologies provide the means for fast, cheap and inclusive experiments.

Numerous contributions in the field of innovation management refer to the importance of organizational *learning*. Modern technologies have a profound influence on the ability of organizations to learn. These are explored in "Organizational learning and the technology of foolishness: the case of virtual worlds at IBM" by Mark Dodgson, David Gann and Nelson Phillips (2013). This study is particularly concerned with 'virtuality': the ability to characterize people, objects and processes by digital representations, and examines the emergence and use of virtual worlds technology in IBM. Virtual worlds were used in meetings, rehearsals and brainstorming. The authors argue organizational learning resulted from forms of *play*. The paper explores how a technology associated with games came to be used in a serious, for-profit company through a process referred to as 'convergent recognition'. Organizational learning results from the interrelated processes behind the adoption of the technology and its application.

The growth of innovation capacity in Asia is the most remarkable transformation to have affected the context for innovation management over the past decade or so. Japanese firms have led innovation practices in numbers of areas for many years, and companies from China, Taiwan, Korea and other Asian nations have recently joined them. To put these developments in broad relief, Mei-Chih Hu and John Mathews (2005) examine "National innovative capacity in East Asia". Using patent analysis (and accepting its shortcomings), these authors explore the development of innovative capability in Taiwan, Korea, Hong Kong, Singapore and China, with more detailed study of Taiwan. They find a different model of development to that found in the OECD (Organisation for Economic Co-operation and Development) nations. Compared to developed economies, these 'catch-up' nations are more involved with technology transfer and the diffusion of 'new to the country' rather than 'new to the world' innovations. Latecomer nations are concerned with the development of their institutional foundations of national innovative capacity, and are more targeted on particular certain industrial sectors, such as information technology and electronics. They also involve greater public investments in R&D. Hu and Mathews argue these policies provide insights into the processes by which latecomers can close the gap with more developed countries.

China's innovative firms are a source of particular interest. Companies such as Huawei, Alibaba and Lenovo have very rapidly become global leaders in innovation. Shulin Gu and Bengt-Åke Lundvall (2006) provide an overview of China's development in innovation and its future challenges in "China's innovation system and the move towards harmonious growth and endogenous innovation". They describe the changes associated with the opening up of China in the 1980s, such as decentralization, privatization and openness, that created an institutional setting that has attracted massive capital accumulation in manufacturing. Further reforms broke down the barriers between the institutions of science and technology and business. Gu and Lundvall show how continued reforms are being seen in the concern to encourage indigenous innovation and 'harmonious development', and argue there is a need for adjustments towards innovation-driven growth and learning-based development. They discuss the continuing shortcomings in the Chinese system of innovation, especially the need for greater interactions between users and producers of knowledge. They argue the need for greater social capital in a segmented society and natural capital in a country beset by environmental challenges.

Zhang (2014) argues the Chinese model of innovation management is strongly influenced by government policies and China's culture, but also through learning from multinational companies and developing their own practices, Chinese approaches to innovation provide an important future direction for the study of innovation management. One of the intriguing insights from Zhang is the distinction between efficiency-led business models in the West and effectiveness-led models in China.

Asia is not the only part of the world to have seen remarkable developments in national innovative capability, and many other countries have seen rapid expansion in this field, albeit with variety in models. Jorge Carrillo and Arturo Lara (2005), in their article "Mexican *maquiladoras*: new capabilities of coordination and the emergence of a new generation of companies", provide an example of a particular model of development and the challenges it poses for companies. *Maquiladoras* are company plants mainly in the car and electronics industries. The authors describe the significance of these firms and the challenges they face. They analyze three generations of these types of company, with different levels of skills, forms of organizing and technological capabilities. Companies have progressed from assembly to manufacturing, from design to research. Using the case of the Delphi Corporation in Juarez, Carrillo and Lara discuss a fourth generation of company. They argue the importance of this fourth generation company that plays a central coordination role in global production chains, and how crucial it is to Mexico's future economic development.

Mirroring to some extent China's concern for harmonious development, there is interest in studying innovation for *inclusive* growth. This concern is the focus of the article by Gerard George, Anita McGahan and Jaideep Prabhu (2012), "Innovation for inclusive growth: towards a theoretical framework and a research agenda". Their attention lies with what organizations can do to engage in social innovation activities to connect disenfranchised individuals and communities with opportunities that foster social and economic growth. Inclusive innovation enfranchises the poor as customers, employees, owners, suppliers and community members. There are numerous examples of very low cost innovations to have emerged from and for poor people, ranging from computers and cars to health care and microfinance. The paper considers theoretical, methodological and empirical issues surrounding inclusive innovation as an introduction to a special edition of the *Journal of Management Studies*. They highlight progress to date in studying this issue, and challenges to be faced, and argue that it is an exciting and important new area of management research.

Lawrence, Dover and Gallagher (1994) refer to the growing interest in managing social innovation, but argue that this growth has not seen a corresponding increase in research in the area. They review the existing literature around four themes that characterize understanding of social innovation: starting with social problems, focusing on novel solutions, varying potential organizing models and benefiting beyond the innovators. They argue future research should recognize the construction of social problems and their historical and social embeddedness, and how the need for political and ethical considerations has to be taken into account.

When studying innovation management it is well to remember Joseph Schumpeter's dictum of innovation being a process of creative destruction. The vast majority of the research into innovation is concerned with its creative elements, with much less addressing its destructive elements. Innovation gives us weapons of mass destruction and the means to pollute ourselves out of existence; it destroys industries, companies, jobs and ways of life; it gives states the ability to control and restrict personal freedoms. It is incumbent on innovation management researchers to study, publicize and whenever possible alleviate the destructive elements of innovation.

Innovation has the potential to accentuate the dangerous social and economic inequalities within and between nations. One of the major societal challenges to be confronted in future, for example, is the effect of modern technologies on the number and quality of jobs, and there are great fears of massive structural unemployment. This is the focus of the books by Erik Brynjolfsson and Andrew McAfee, *Race Against the Machine* (2012) and *The Second Machine Age* (2014). Brynjolfsson and McAfee pose the question of what will happen as technology continues to replace increasing numbers of humans. They develop a widespread agenda for action, and innovation management researchers in future would be advised to engage with this critically important debate. Technology and innovation results from the actions of humans, and concern for their human consequences should be first and foremost in the mind of those who can influence their development, such as those working in the field of innovation management.

Innovation management research is, overall, in a strong position. The field of innovation management is being progressively recognized in universities in business, engineering and design schools. There are increasing numbers of academic journals dedicated to the area, and more articles on the subject are appearing in mainstream management and business journals. There is a healthy number of textbooks and research monographs in the field. With over 3,000 members, the Technology and Innovation Management Division is the sixth largest of the 25 divisions in the American Academy of Management (and if it were to be combined with Entrepreneurship, it would be the largest).

Several issues will need to be addressed for this strong trajectory to continue. First, the pressures on the research community to produce *quantity* of research publications has to change to focus on their *quality*. University incentive systems, driven by government policies and research ranking metrics, are not encouraging the long-term research and thinking necessary to advance the field. There is far too much research being published that may meet the process requirements deemed necessary but are virtually devoid of interesting content and findings. Second, more innovation management researchers need to be engaging with cutting-edge practices in firms and organizations. The subject changes quickly – witness the impact of digital innovation technologies – and useful research is based on understanding how innovation is actively managed. A corollary of this engagement is that more innovation management researchers should be actively engaged with changing and improving practice. Third, more diverse and adventurous research methods are needed. Big data and artificial intelligence will produce many more exciting opportunities for insights from novel data sources, and unless innovation management researchers avail themselves of these techniques, others, potentially from the sciences, will be delivering the important insights. Fourth, research has to expand beyond its focus on the United States and Europe. Many of the most interesting and influential developments in the field will be found elsewhere in the future, in Asia, India, Latin America, and potentially in Africa. Innovation is a truly global phenomenon, and this should be reflected in its study.

References

Abernathy, W. and Utterback, J. (1975), A dynamic model of process and product innovation, *Omega*, 3,6: 639–656.

Acs, Z. and Audretsch, D. (1988), Innovation in large and small firms: An empirical analysis, *American Economic Review*, 78,4: 678–690.

Adams, R., Bessant, J. and Phelps, R. (2006), Innovation management measurement: A review, *International Journal of Management Reviews*, 8,1: 21–47.

Ahuja, G. (2000), Collaboration networks, structural holes and innovation: A longitudinal study, *Administrative Science Quarterly*, 45,3: 425–455.

Ahuja, G. and Katila, R. (2001), Technological acquisitions and the innovation performance of acquiring firms: A longitudinal study, *Strategic Management Journal*, 22: 197–220.

Ahuja, G. and Lampert, C. (2001), Entrepreneurship in the large corporation: A longitudinal study of how established firms create breakthrough innovations, *Strategic Management Journal*, 22,6/7: 521–543.

Arora, A. and Gambardella, A. (2010), Ideas for rent: An overview of markets for technology, *Industrial and Corporate Change*, 19: 775–803.

Arthur, B. (1990), Positive feedbacks in the economy, *Scientific American*, February: 80–85.

Atuahene-Gima, K. (2005), Resolving the capability – Rigidity paradox in new product innovation, *Journal of Marketing*, 69,4: 61–83.

Barley, S. (1998), What can we learn from the history of technology? *Journal of Engineering Technology Management*, 15: 237–255.

Berkhout, F. (2014), Sustainable innovation management, in *The Oxford Handbook of Innovation Management*, Oxford, Oxford University Press.

Berkhout, F., Hertin, J. and Gann, D. (2006), Learning to adapt: Organisational adaptation to climate change impacts, *Climatic Change*, 78: 135–156.

Brynjolfsson, E. and McAfee, A. (2012), *Race Against the Machine*, Lexington, Digital Frontier Press.

Brynjolfsson, E. and McAfee, A. (2014), *The Second Machine Age*, New York, Norton.

Burns, T. and Stalker, G. M. (1961), *The Management of Innovation*, London, Tavistock Publications: 1–14.

Burt, R. (2004), Structural holes and good ideas, *American Journal of Sociology*, 110,1: 349–399.

Carrillo, J. and Lara, A. (2005), Mexican maquiladoras: New capabilities of coordination and the emergence of a new generation of companies, *Innovation: Management, Policy and Practice*, 7,2: 256–273.

Chesbrough, H. (2003), Introduction, in *Open Innovation*, Boston, Harvard Business School Press: xvii–xxxi.

Chesbrough, H. and Rosenbloom, R. (2002), The role of the business model in capturing value from innovation: Evidence from Xerox Corporation's technology spin-off companies, *Industrial and Corporate Change*, 11,3: 529–555.

Christensen, C. (1997), How can great firms fail? in Chapter 1, *The Innovator's Dilemma*, Boston, Harvard University Press: 3–28.

Clark, K. and Wheelwright, S. (1992), Organizing and leading 'heavyweight' development teams, *California Management Review*, 34,3: 9–28.

Cohen, W. and Levinthal, D. (1994), Fortune favors the prepared firm, *Management Science*, 40,2: 227–251.

Conceição, P., Hamill, D. and Pinheiro, P. (2002), Innovative science and technology commercialization strategies at 3M: A case study, *Journal of Engineering Technology Management*, 19: 25–38.

Cooper, R. (2005), A world-class *stage gate®* idea-to-launch framework for your business, in Chapter 7, *Product Leadership*, New York, Basic Books: 200–237.

Dahlander, L. and Gann, D. (2010), How open is innovation? *Research Policy*, 39,6: 699–709.

David, P. (1985), Clio and the economics of QWERTY, *Economic History*, 75,2: 332–337.

Davies, A., Gann, D. and Douglas, T. (2009), Innovation in megaprojects: Systems integration at London Heathrow Terminal 5, *California Management Review*, 51,2: 101–125.

Davies, A. and Mackenzie, I. (2013), Project complexity and systems integration: Constructing the London 2012 Olympics and Paralympics Games, *International Journal of Project Management*, 32,5.

De Solla Price, D. (1984), The science/technology relationship, the craft of experimental science, and policy for the improvement of high technology innovation, *Research Policy*, 12: 1.

Dodgson, M. (2011), Exploring new combinations in innovation and entrepreneurship: Social networks, Schumpeter, and the case of Josiah Wedgwood (1730–1795), *Industrial and Corporate Change*, 20,4: 1119–1151.

Dodgson, M. (2014), Collaboration and innovation management, in *The Oxford Handbook of Innovation Management*, Oxford, Oxford University Press.

Dodgson, M., Gann, D., MacAulay, S. and Davies, A. (2015), Innovation strategy in new transportation systems: The case of Crossrail, *Transportation Research Part A: Policy and Practice*, 77: 261–275.

Dodgson, M., Gann, D. and Phillips, N. (2013), Organizational learning and the technology of foolishness: The case of virtual worlds in IBM, *Organization Science*, 24,5: 1358–1376.

Dodgson, M., Gann, D. and Phillips, N. (2014), Perspectives on innovation management, in *The Oxford Handbook of Innovation Management*, Oxford, Oxford University Press.

Dodgson, M., Gann, D. and Salter, A. (2005), *Think, Play, Do: Technology, Innovation and Organization*, Oxford, Oxford University Press.

Dodgson, M., Gann, D. and Salter, A. (2006), The role of technology in the shift towards open innovation: The case of Procter & Gamble, *R&D Management*, 36,3: 333–346.

Dodgson, M., Gann, D. and Salter, A. (2007), 'In case of fire, please use the elevator': Simulation technology and organization in fire engineering, *Organization Science*, 18,5: 849–864.

Dolfsma, W. (2004), The process of new service development – Issues of formalization and appropriability, *International Journal of Innovation Management*, 8,3: 319–337.

Dosi, G. (1982), Technological paradigms and technological trajectories, *Research Policy*, 11: 147–162.

Drucker, P. (1985), The discipline of innovation, *Harvard Business Review*, May–June: 67–72.

Freeman, C. (1994), The economics of technical change, *Cambridge Journal of Economics*, 18: 463–514.

Freeman, C. (1995), The 'national system of innovation' in historical perspective, *Cambridge Journal of Economics*, 19: 5–24.

Gardiner, P. and Rothwell, R. (1988), Re-innovation and robust designs: Producer and user benefits, *Journal of Marketing Management*, 3,3: 372–387.

Gawer, A. and Cusumano, M. (2002), *Platform Leadership*, Boston, Harvard Business School Press: 245–269.

George, G., McGahan, A. and Prabhu, J. (2012), Innovation for inclusive growth: Towards a theoretical framework and a research agenda, *Journal of Management Studies*, 49,4: 661–683.

Gibbons, M. and Johnston, R. (1974), The roles of science in technological innovation, *Research Policy*, 3: 220–242.

Granstrand, O. and Sjölander, S. (1990), Managing innovation in multi-technology corporations, *Research Policy*, 19,1: 35–60.

Gu, S. and Lundvall, B.-A. (2006), China's innovation system and the move toward harmonious growth and endogenous innovation, *Innovation: Management, Policy and Practice*, 8,1–2: 1–26.

Hargadon, A. and Douglas, Y. (2001), When innovations meet institutions: Edison and the design of the electric light, *Administrative Science Quarterly*, 46,3: 476–501.

Hargadon, A. and Sutton, R. (1997), Technology brokering and innovation in a product development firm, *Administrative Science Quarterly*, 44,4: 716–749.

Henderson, R. and Clark, K. (1990), Architectural innovation: The reconfiguration of existing product technologies and the failure of established firms, *Administrative Science Quarterly*, 35,1: 9–30.

Hu, M.-C. and Mathews, J. (2005), National innovative capacity in East Asia, *Research Policy*, 34,9: 1322–1349.

Hughes, A. (2014), Capital markets, innovation systems, and the financing of innovation, in *The Oxford Handbook of Innovation Management*, Oxford, Oxford University Press.

Jeppesen, L. and Frederiksen, L. (2006), Why do users contribute to firm-hosted user communities? The case of computer-controlled music instruments, *Organization Science*, 17,1: 45–63.

Kastelle, T. and Steen, J. (2014), Networks of innovation, in *The Oxford Handbook of Innovation Management*, Oxford, Oxford University Press.

Katz, R. and Allen, T. (1985), Project performance and the locus of influence in the R&D matrix, *Academy of Management Journal*, 28,1: 67–87.

Kogut, B. and Zander, U. (2000), Did socialism fail to innovate? A natural experiment of the two Zeiss companies, *American Sociological Review*, 65,2: 169–190.

Kuhn, T. (1962), *The Structure of Scientific Revolutions*, Chicago, Chicago University Press.

Laursen, K. and Salter, A. (2006), Open for innovation: The role of openness in explaining innovation performance among U.K. manufacturing firms, *Strategic Management Journal*, 27,2: 131–150.

Lawrence, T., Dover, G. and Gallagher, B. (1994), Managing social innovation, in *The Oxford Handbook of Innovation Management*, Oxford, Oxford University Press.

Leiponen, A. (2008), Competing through cooperation: Standard setting in wireless telecommunications, *Management Science*, 54,11: 1904–1919.

Leonard-Barton, D. (1992), Core capabilities and core rigidities: A paradox in managing new product development, *Strategic Management Journal*, 13,1: 111–125.

Maidique, M. (1980), Entrepreneurs, champions and technological innovation, *Sloan Management Review*, 2: 59–76.

Mansfield, E. (1991), Academic research and industrial innovation, *Research Policy*, 20,1: 1–12.

Malerba, F. and Adams, P. (2014), Sectoral Systems of Innovation, in Dodgson, M., Gann, D. and Phillips, N., *The Oxford Handbook of Innovation Management*, Oxford, Oxford University Press.

March, J. (1991), Exploration and exploitation in organizational learning, *Organization Science*, 2,1: 71–87.

Mokyr, J. (1990), China and Europe, in Chapter 6, *The Lever of Riches: Technological Creativity and Economic Progress*, New York, Oxford University Press: 209–238.

Morison, E. (1988), Gunfire at sea: A case study of innovation, in M. Tushman and W. Moore (eds.), *Readings in the Management of Innovation*, New York, Harper Collins: 165–178.

Nelson, R. and Winter, S. (1982), *An Evolutionary Theory of Technical Change*, Cambridge, MA, Belknap Press.

Nielsen, M. (2012), *Reinventing Discovery: The New Era of Networked Science*, Princeton, Princeton University Press.

Osterwalder, A., Pigneur, Y. and Tucci, C. (2005), Clarifying business models: Origins, present, and future of the concept, *Communications of the Association for Information Systems*, 16: 1–25.

Pavitt, K. (1990), What we know about the strategic management of technology, *California Management Review*, 32,3: 17–26.

Pavitt, K. (1991), Key characteristics of the large innovating firm, *British Journal of Management*, 2: 41–50.

Powell, W., Koput, K. and Smith-Doerr, L. (1996), Interorganizational collaboration and the locus of learning: Networks of learning in biotechnology, *Administrative Science Quarterly*, 41,1: 116–145.

Reagans, R. and McEvily, B. (2003), Network structure and knowledge transfer: The effects of cohesion and range, *Administrative Science Quarterly*, 48,2: 240–267.

Rogers, E. (1995), Attributes of innovations and their rate of adoption, in Chapter 6, *Diffusion of Innovations*, 4th Edition, New York, Free Press: 204–251.

Rosenberg, N. (1990), Why do firms do basic research (with their own money)? *Research Policy*, 19: 165–174.

Rosenbloom, R. and Cusumano, M. (1987), Technological pioneering and competitive advantage: The birth of the VCR industry, *California Management Review*, 29,4: 51–76.

Rothwell, R. (1994), Towards the 5th generation innovation process, *International Marketing Review*, 11,1: 7–31.

Rothwell, R. and Dodgson, M. (1994), Innovation and size of firm, in M. Dodgson and R. Rothwell (eds.), *The Handbook of Industrial Innovation*, Cheltenham, Edward Elgar.

Rothwell, R., Freeman, C., Horsley, A., Jervis, V., Robertson, A. and Townsend, J. (1974), SAPPHO updated – Project SAPPHO phase I, *Research Policy*, 3: 258–291.

Schilling, M. (2005), Protecting innovation, in Chapter 9, *Strategic Management of Technological Innovation*, New York, McGraw Hill: 165–185.

Schnaars, S. (1994), The elements of imitation, in Chapter 1, *Managing Imitation Strategies*, New York, Free Press: 5–14.

Schumpeter, J. (1934), *The Theory of Economic Development*, Cambridge, MA, Harvard University Press.

Schumpeter, J. (1942), *Capitalism, Socialism and Democracy*, New York, Harper.

Takeuchi, H. and Nonaka, I. (1986), The new product development game, *Harvard Business Review*, January–February: 137–146.

Teece, D. (1986), Profiting from technological innovation: Implications for integration, collaboration, licensing and public policy, *Research Policy*, 15,6: 285–305.

Teece, D., Pisano, G. and Shuen, A. (1997), Dynamic capabilities and strategic management, *Strategic Management Journal*, 18,7: 509–533.

Tellis, G., Prabhu, J. and Chandy, R. (2009), Radical innovation across nations: The preeminence of corporate culture, *Journal of Marketing*, 73,1: 3–23.

Tether, B. (2014), Services, Innovation, and Managing Services Innovation, in Dodgson, M., Gann, D., and Phillips, N. *The Oxford Handbook of Innovation Management*, Oxford, Oxford University Press.

Tushman, M. and Anderson, P. (1986), Technological discontinuities and organizational environments, *Administrative Science Quarterly*, 31,3: 439–465.

Tushman, M. and O'Reilly, A. (1996), The ambidextrous organization: Managing evolutionary and revolutionary change, *California Management Review*, 38: 1–23.

Utterback, J. (1994), The dynamics of innovation in industry, in Chapter 1, *Mastering the Dynamics of Innovation*, Boston, Harvard Business School Press: 1–21.

Van de Ven, A. (1986), Central problems in the management of innovation, *Management Science*, 32,5: 590–607.

Verganti, R. (2008), Design, meanings, and radical innovation: A metamodel and a research agenda, *Journal of Product Innovation Management*, 25,5: 436–456.

Von Hippel, E. (1986), Lead users: A source of novel product concepts, *Management Science*, 32,7: 791–805.

Von Hippel, E. (1994), 'Sticky information' and the locus of problem solving: Implications for innovation, *Management Science*, 40,4: 429–439.

Von Hippel, E. (2005), Innovation communities, in Chapter 7, *Democratizing Innovation*, Cambridge, MA, MIT Press: 93–106.

Von Tunzelmann, N., Malerba, F., Nightingale, P. and Metcalfe, S. (2008), Technological paradigms, past, present and future, *Industrial and Corporate Change*, 17,3: 467–484.

Zhang, M. (2014), Innovation management in China, in M. Dodgson, D. Gann and N. Phillips (eds.), *The Oxford Handbook of Innovation Management*, Oxford, Oxford University Press: 355–374.

Index

3M 42

Abernathy, W. 12
absorptive capacity 14
academic research: and innovation
4, 38–39; long-term 61; problem-
solving in 39–40; social returns
from 39
Acs, Z. 40–41
Adams, P. 12
Adams, R. 48
adaptation 27
Ahuja, G. 41–42, 44–45, 47–48
Alibaba 58
Allen, T. 46
analogies 45
Anderson, P. 24
applied research 34
appropriability regimes 13
architectural innovation 23–24
Arora, A. 33
Arrow, K. 30
Arthur, B. 9
artificial intelligence (AI) 34–35
Arup 57
Asia: innovation capacity in 57–58;
research and development investments
58; technology transfer in 58
Atuahene-Gima, K. 46
Audretsch, D. 40–41
automotive industry 12
autonomous development teams 30

Barley, S. 43
basic research 33–34

Bell Labs 55
Berkhout, F. 53–54
Bessant, J. 48
biotechnology 12
boundary objects 57
Brynjolfsson, E. 60
Burns, T. 16–17
Burt, R. 25–26
business models 43, 52, 59

capitalism 19
Carrillo, J. 59
champions 30
Chandy, R. 47
Chesbrough, H. 43, 55
China: effectiveness-led business
models 59; and incentives 20;
innovation capacity in 57–58;
manufacturing in 58; technological
innovation in 20
Christensen, C. 27
Cisco 55
Clark, K. 23–24, 29
climate change 53–54
closed innovation 55
Cohen, W. 14
collaboration 30–31
compatibility 15
competence-destroying technology
discontinuities 24
competence-enhancing technology
discontinuities 24
competitive advantage 33, 40
competitors: and appropriability regimes
13; and complementary assets 13

Printed in the United States
by Baker & Taylor Publisher Services